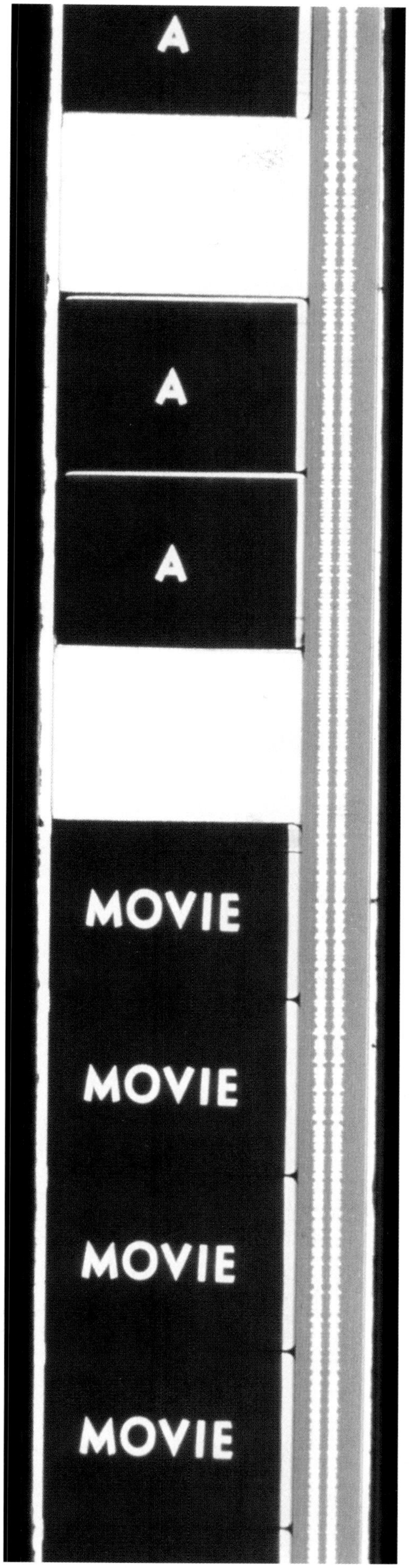
A
A
A
MOVIE
MOVIE
MOVIE
MOVIE

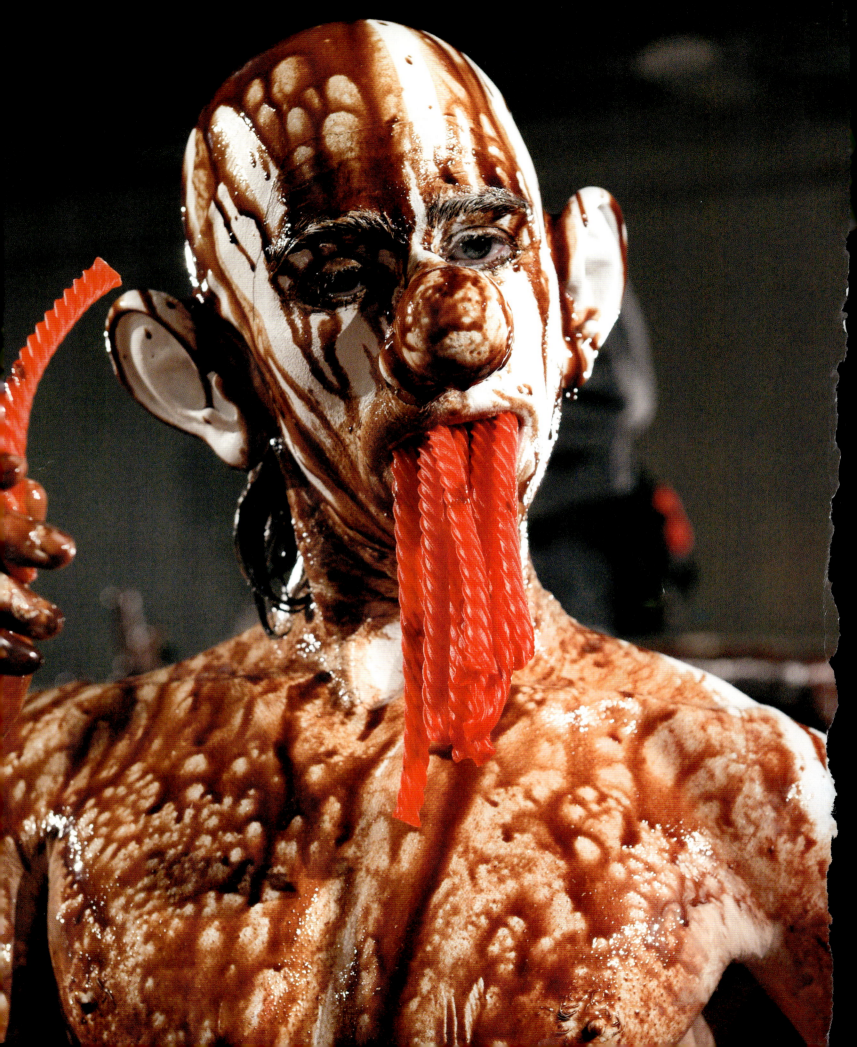

Paul Young / Paul Duncan (Ed.)

ART CINEMA

TASCHEN

HONG KONG KÖLN LONDON LOS ANGELES MADRID PARIS TOKYO

FRONT AND BACK COVER
Film strips from 'Death of the Gorilla' (1965–66)
Peter Mays created this hypnotic film by shooting scenes off a television set and transforming them into a dense, layered collage.

FIRST PAGE
Film strip from 'A Movie' (1958)
Bruce Conner's first collage film—made entirely out of found footage—was initially meant to play inside a piece of sculpture he devised for a gallery, but quickly took on a life of its own. It deftly weaves together an array of chase sequences before exploding into a cavalcade of disaster scenes. More importantly, it bears Conner's unmistakable knack for subtle rhythms and outright irony.

FRONTISPIECE
Still from 'Caribbean Pirates' (2001–2005)

THIS SPREAD
Still from 'Confessions of a Black Mother Succuba' (1965)
California's Robert Nelson was part of the funk movement in the early 1960s, and, as such, often enjoyed the collision between high and low culture. Thus, with this freewheeling, satirical take on pop culture, he places both found and original material (including staged erotica) into unexpected juxtapositions, which create new, unexpected meanings.

PAGES 6/7
Still from 'Crack Brutal Grief' (2000)
As a leading figure of Canada's experimental-video scene, Bruce Elder fuses philosophy with digital software to create moving, semiabstract works. For this piece, he synthesized images culled entirely from the web to create a dreamlike study of human malfeasance.

To stay informed about upcoming TASCHEN titles, please request our magazine at www.taschen.com/magazine or write to TASCHEN America, 6671 Sunset Boulevard, Suite 1508, Los Angeles, CA 90028, USA, contact-us@taschen.com, Fax: +1-323-463.4442. We will be happy to send you a free copy of our magazine, which is filled with information about all of our books.

© 2009 TASCHEN GmbH
Hohenzollernring 53, D–50672 Köln
www.taschen.com
Editor: Paul Duncan/Wordsmith Solutions
Editorial Coordination: Martin Holz, Cologne
Production Coordination: Martina Ciborowius, Cologne
Typeface Design: Sense/Net, Andy Disl and Birgit Eichwede, Cologne

Printed in China
ISBN 978–3–8228–3594–4

Acknowledgments and Special Thanks
Thank you to Damon Young for technical assistance, Jordan Halsey for design work, Steve Anker for his continual support and for reading my text, Steven Jenkins from the San Francisco Cinematheque for his support and contacts, Cindy Keefer from the Center for Visual Music for her insight, Rani Singh for introducing me to P. Adams, Severin Wonderman for his help, Adam Hyman for his great programming and contacts, Henriette Huldish and Chrissie Iles at the Whitney for their early support, and Laurence Kardish, Barbara London, and Paul Power at MoMA for their time. I would also like to thank the numerous artists who provided me with interviews, access to their work, and images, including Bruce Baillie, Craig Baldwin, Judith Barry, Steve Beck, Pierre Bismuth, Robert Breer, Abigail Child, Sue Costabile, Nick Dorsky, Stan Douglas, Jeffers Egan, Harun Farocki, Janice Findley, Henry Flynt, David Gatten, Ernie Gehr, Janie Geiser, Barry Gerson, Larry Gottheim, Robert Haller, Kevin Hanley, Lynn Hershman Leeson, Teresa Hubbard and Alexander Birchler, Tak Iimura, Ken Jacobs, Alejandro Jodorowsky, Lew Klahr, Peter Kubelka, David Larcher, David Lebrun, Paul McCarthy, Chris Marker, Jonas Mekas, Sarah Morris, Matthias Müller, Richard Myers, Andrew Noren, Pat O'Neill, Gunvor Nelson, Osbert Parker, Jeff Perkins, Paulette Phillips, Nicolas Provost, Al Razutis, Jürgen Reble, Jay Rosenblatt, Julia Scher, Christopher Sharits, Carolee Schneemann, Michael Snow, Phil Solomon, Peter Tscherkassky, Steina and Woody Vasulka, Marnie Weber, Chris Welsby, Robert Wilson, and John Whitney Jr.

CONTENTS

8   INTRODUCTION   What is 'Art Cinema'?

18   PART ONE   Surrealist Cinema

36   PART TWO   Post-Surrealism and the Mythopoeic

50   PART THREE   Abstraction and the Lyrical Film

68   PART FOUR   The City Symphony, the Essay, and the Landscape Film

88   PART FIVE   Temps Mort, Tableau, and Duration

104   PART SIX   Structuralism and the Conceptual Film

116   PART SEVEN   Expanded Cinema and the Installation Film

132   PART EIGHT   Collage and the Found-Footage Film

148   PART NINE   Portraiture and Autobiography

166   PART TEN   Dada, Parody, Camp, and the Remake

188   CHRONOLOGY

190   FILMOGRAPHY

191   BIBLIOGRAPHY

What is 'Art Cinema'?

To paraphrase U.S. Supreme Court Associate Justice Potter Stewart's summation of pornography, it may be difficult to define, but you'll probably know it when you see it.

Generally speaking, an art film—whether it falls under the heading of experimental, avant-garde, or artist's film—is a film that sets itself apart from commercial, mainstream fare through aesthetic, ideological, and/or political means. As the preeminent scholar and avant-garde historian P. Adams Sitney writes, "the precise relationship of the avant-garde cinema to the American commercial film is one of radical otherness. They operate in different realms with next to no significant influence on each other."

But just because the avant-garde operates in opposition to the mainstream, it would be inappropriate to say that commercial cinema is unartistic. After all, a quick survey of European, Latin American, and Asian cinemas alone would prove that commercial filmmakers are prone to using avant-garde techniques, and they often do so with great success.

Of course, American cinema is a reflection of American aesthetics, which has always valued realism and straightforwardness. As Donald Richie writes, "[in American cinema] nothing is left fragmentary, open, or half-illuminated; never a lacuna, never a glimpse of unplumbed depths." By contrast, the art film tends to lean toward the non-linear, non-theatrical, and non-figurative, which means it operates largely through poetics, metaphor, and allusion. While that may sound like a recipe for boredom (and it can be), it can also be extraordinarily affecting. Hollywood may have mastered the most visceral form of cinema, where sound, editing, and story come together to create a powerful, albeit manipulative, viewing experience, but the art film has mastered another kind of power—that of the image itself. And when it works, as it often does, it can outstrip Hollywood pyrotechnics by far.

To fully appreciate this genre, which has often escaped both cinematic and art-historical surveys, one must understand that it requires a different kind of viewing altogether. Like traditional artworks, art films are generally open-ended and offer questions rather than answers. That means the viewer is free to inject him- or herself more fully into the process and experience the work at a deeper level. As the late filmmaker Paul Sharits once said, the experience is a bit like "listening with one's eyes."

Still from 'Brazil' (1985)
Terry Gilliam has often drawn from surrealist methods of juxtaposition in his mainstream films, but rarely as much as he did with this film. Here he uses expressive set design to tell an absurdist tale of a future society where the inhabitants can't remember how—or why—they should rebel.

"The cinema has to be destroyed."
Guy Debord

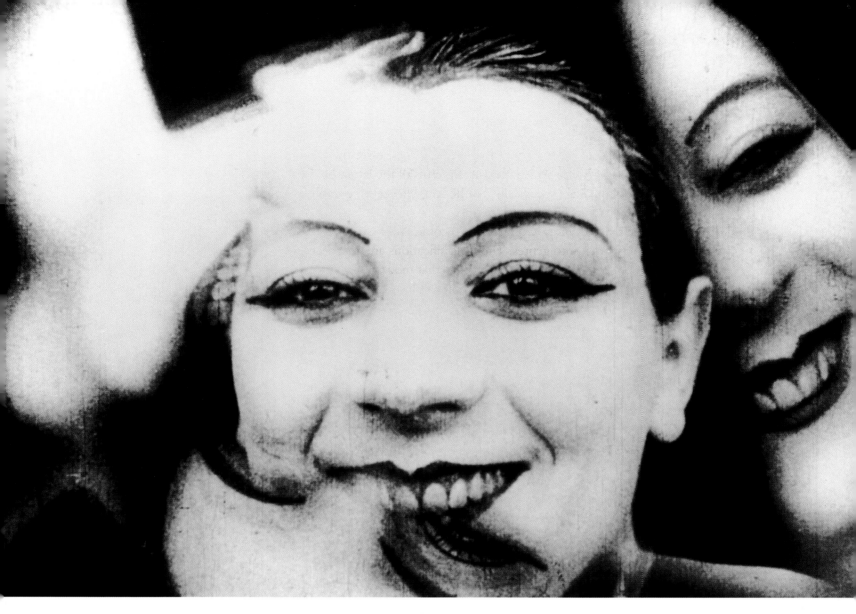

ABOVE
Still from 'Ballet mécanique' (1924)
Being part of the burgeoning modernist art scene of the early 1920s, painter Fernand Léger worked with the American filmmaker Dudley Murphy and the composer George Antheil to create a playful study of contrasts between machinery and the human form.

LEFT
Still from 'La folie du Docteur Tube' (1915)
This early film by France's Abel Gance anticipates the experimental-film scene of the postwar period by telling the tale of a mad doctor who inhales a white powder and hallucinates impossible scenarios.

But that only tells half the story. Because the art film also has another trajectory, one that defines the work less in terms of its ability to induce intense cinematic experiences, and more in terms of its place as a discrete art object. Peter Wollen touched on that idea when he wrote his 1975 essay "The Two Avant-Gardes," which basically suggests that there is a film avant-garde that stresses signification, language, and codes (à la 1970s Jean-Luc Godard) and another that stresses the physical material of film and the space in which it exists. In terms of the latter, he was speaking of structuralist filmmakers specifically, but he could have just as easily been discussing the entire range of art films made specifically for gallery settings.

This book groups a wide range of films—from shorts to commercial narratives; from video art to installation works—into genres. These classifications are not meant to be absolute. Rather they are best seen as basic techniques that reoccur in various mediums, eras, and nationalities. Many were coined by Sitney in his groundbreaking 1974 text, *Visionary Film: The American Avant-Garde*, but here you will also find forays into duration, the tableau, found footage, the installation film, the city symphony, portraiture, parody, and camp.

Limited space means the exclusion of several important genres, however, including realism, expressionism, experimental animation, web-based works, and, most regrettably, a large number of international and third world cinemas. I tried to include as many European, Latin American, and Asian films as I could, but there is no denying the fact that this book has an American bent. That is only because I prefer to write about films that I have seen or know about.

Nonetheless, this is an uncommonly comprehensive study, with hundreds of films and filmmakers represented. My goal is to shed some light on what is generally believed to be a very small practice that only sees the light of day in basements, art-house cinemas, galleries, and "specialty screenings." But, in fact, the art film is a massive, worldwide phenomenon of immense scope—so large, in fact, that it extends far beyond the reach of this book. After all, there are now more art films than at any time in history, with thousands being made each and every day. And with the recent advances in digital technologies, enhanced interactivity, game theory, and much more, we are currently on the verge of a worldwide revolution in the cinematic arts, one that may dwarf the introduction of sound by unknown proportions. Celluloid will likely be the first casualty, of course, but what will emerge will undoubtedly challenge and complement the entire history of film.

But should we still call it cinema?

The film artist Anthony McCall may have answered that question best when he argued that "we tend to talk interchangeably, and not very usefully, about film and cinema, as if they were the same thing. Cinema is a social institution, while film is a medium … And I can quite easily imagine film as a medium disappearing quietly in the next 10 years with scarcely a blip in terms of the *practice* of cinema. Whereas the institution will be just fine."

"Hurray for the formless film: a non-literary, non-musical picture film that doesn't tell a story, become an abstract dance, or deliver a message; a film where words are pictures and sounds skip around like thoughts do."
Robert Breer

Still from 'Ballet mécanique' (1924)

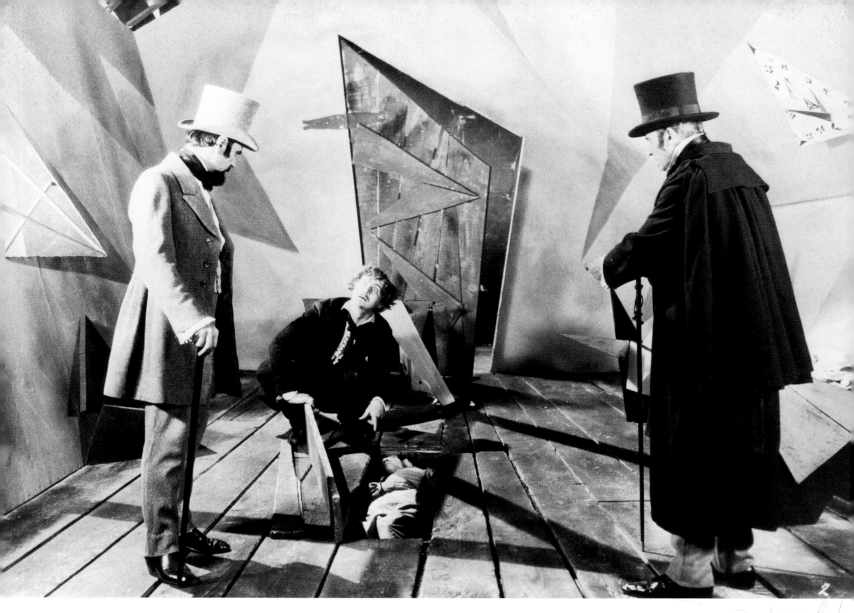

ABOVE
Still from 'The Telltale Heart' (1928)
Charles Klein's film is said to be the first cinematic adaptation of Edgar Allan Poe's famous short story, which follows the paranoid delusions of a narrator who believes that the remains of the man he murdered have come alive under his floorboards. Klein's approach remains faithful to Poe's original, yet without the crutch of dialogue the film relies on set design and montage to convey tone.

LEFT
Still from 'J'accuse!' (1919)
Known as a restless innovator, Abel Gance toned down his radical experimentation for this, his 22nd film, which tells the story of a man who falls in love with a friend's wife.

ABOVE
Still from 'The Fall of the House of Usher' (1928)
James Sibley Watson and Melville Webber
were pioneers in avant-garde practices, and
routinely employed expressionistic set designs
and innovative montage techniques for their
expressionistic films. Here they worked with
poet e.e. cummings to bring Poe's story to the
screen, but the film is best known for their use
of repetition and rhyming structures.

RIGHT
**Still from 'The Good, the Bad and the Ugly'
('Il buono, il brutto, il cattivo', 1966)**
While ostensibly about three killers on convergent
paths to find a stash of gold, in this film director
Sergio Leone epitomizes his interest in formal
composition and graphic storytelling.

ABOVE AND OPPOSITE
Stills from 'The Way' (1929)
The American-born photographer Francis Bruguière was a contemporary of Man Ray, but failed to receive the same recognition. He was also deeply interested in cinema and produced a handful of evocative abstract experiments, such as this unfinished project involving distortion mirrors and nude female forms.

"For alchemy to take place in a film, the form must include the expression of its own materiality, and this materiality must be in union with its subject matter. If the union is not present, if the film's literalness is so overwhelming, so illustrative, it obliterates the medium it's composed of."

Nathaniel Dorsky

THIS PAGE AND OPPOSITE BOTTOM
Stills from 'The Battleship Potemkin'
('Bronyenosyets Potyomkin', 1925)
While meant to be one of a series of propaganda films detailing key moments in Russia's revolution, *The Battleship Potemkin* also served as director Sergei Eisenstein's most potent vehicle for his theory of montage. The entire film consists of contrasts and juxtapositions, which are designed to manipulate the audience for maximum effect.

ABOVE
Production still from 'The Battleship Potemkin'
('Bronyenosyets Potyomkin', 1925)
Director Sergei Eisenstein.

Surrealist Cinema

The surrealist movement is generally associated with a brief period spanning the years between World War I and World War II. Yet its techniques and effects were so profound that it continues to be one of the most durable and provocative genres of art filmmaking worldwide.

Inspired by the Zurich Dada movement of the early 1900s, surrealism proper was spawned by the collision between Dada's best-known visual artists and a group of Paris-based writers and poets, which included André Breton, Robert Desnos, Paul Éluard, and Louis Aragon.

Collectively, these artists were in revolt against the rationalism of the Enlightenment, the boorishness of the bourgeoisie, and the sheer failure of traditional art forms to probe deeper into the furthest reaches of the mind. Thus their aim was essentially romantic. For them, art—and humankind—should reestablish links with the "primal mind," meaning a mind totally free from social conventions, morals, or traditions. To that end, the surrealists not only explored verbal spontaneity (automatism), but all sorts of mind-expansion techniques, including lucid dreaming, sleep deprivation, acute mania, dementia, and intoxication of every conceivable sort. "One of surrealism's points of departure," writes Jean Goudal, "is the observation that everything that emerges from the mind, even without logical form, inevitably reveals the singularity of that mind."

Thus their artworks deliberately trafficked in—and were the physical manifestation of—raw emotions, unbridled thoughts, and the deepest desires. As Mark Gould writes, "surrealist art is desire made solid. For the goal of surrealism is to give birth to truly provocative images, ones that might be too much for the rational mind to digest."

Luis Buñuel and Salvador Dalí achieved just that with their 16-minute short film, *Un chien andalou* (1929). They composed the film entirely through a series of free-association exercises that were as rigorous as they were radical: Any image that could be attributed to a remembrance or a specific cultural/mythical source was rejected outright. As a result, the film traffics entirely in the irrational and the illogical, yet still manages to have a semicoherent through-line thanks to the use of Richard Wagner's *Tristan and Isolde*. Many critics, in fact, have found clear Freudian themes at play, despite the filmmakers' attempts to reject any obvious interpretations. The now-famous sequence inside the apartment, where a lustful

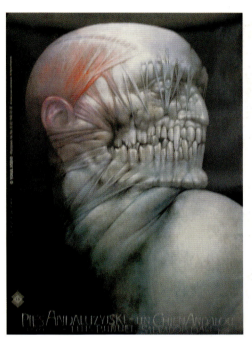

ABOVE
Polish poster for 'Un chien andalou' (1929)

OPPOSITE
Still from 'Caribbean Pirates' (2001–2005)

"The cinema is a marvelous and dangerous weapon if a free spirit wields it."
Luis Buñuel

Still from 'La course aux potirons' (1908)
One of the first animators in the history of cinema, France's Émile Cohl rarely told linear stories. Instead he would allow his characters to continually morph into unexpected incarnations, which gave them a surrealist edge. Here he mixes live action and stop-motion photography to animate a pumpkin race.

Still from 'La cigarette' (1919)
An early film by France's pioneer female director, Germaine Dulac. Like all of her films, it subverts convention and transforms a sentimental melodrama into a cine-poem with deep psychological and subjective references.

ABOVE
Still from 'Paris qui dort' (1925)
René Clair's silent short tells the story of a caretaker who awakens one morning to find that everyone in Paris has either vanished or turned into a statue. As a result some have called it the first end-of-the-world film.

RIGHT
Still from 'Le coquille et le clergyman' (1928)
Germaine Dulac was a pioneer of the cine-poem, which concentrates more on literary and symbolic associations than on plot devices. For this film she used the story of a priest's struggle with his own lustful urges to experiment with atmosphere and fantasy sequences.

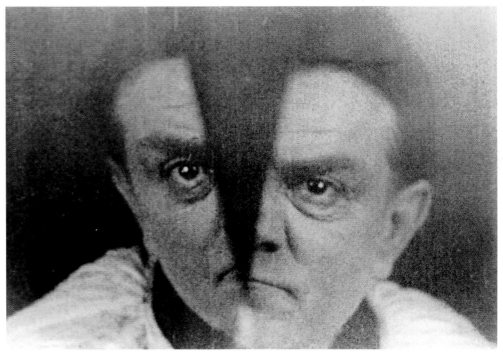

ABOVE
Still from 'The Great Blondino' (1967)
Inspired by one of William T. Wiley's paintings of the French daredevil Blondin, Wiley and Robert Nelson created this masterful pseudonarrative that follows a Buster Keaton–esque protagonist overcoming an array of absurd obstacles. This occasionally tips the film into surreal territory, as in this moment at the zoo.

[handwritten notes:] Jean Cocteau ('The Blood of a Poet' ('Le Sang d'un Poète') 1930) - feature film follows hallucinations of an artist who got lost in his own creativity

have a look (especially on J. Jakubisko)

OPPOSITE
Stills from 'The Cage' (1947)
In this playful short, beat poet and filmmaker Sidney Peterson follows the adventures of a detached retina as it rolls through the streets of San Francisco. The effect is comedic and somewhat surreal, but also a metaphor for the insatiable curiosity of the beats.

husband charges after his terrified wife but finds his arms tied to a pair of grand pianos draped with rotting mules, which in turn are tied to a pair of bewildered priests, can be read as the rejection of sexual urges by both cultural and moral means. Yet for Dalí and Buñuel, the scene was simply meant to be bombastic. As Dalí later said, "I had understood that the point [of surrealism] was to transcribe thought spontaneously, without any rational, aesthetic, or moral checks."

Un chien andalou inspired a legion of filmmakers worldwide, but surrealism itself came to an end by 1930 as the original members disbanded. Nonetheless, the movement found new adherents in the United States in the 1950s and 1960s, most notably in the wildly inventive films of Sidney Peterson (*The Lead Shoes*, 1949), Ian Hugo (*Bells of Atlantis*, 1952), Stan VanDerBeek (*Breathdeath*, 1964), and Richard Myers (*First Time Here*, 1964). Even the avant-garde pioneers Hans Richter and Jean Cocteau came to the States to direct their deliberately surrealist effort, *8 x 8: A Chess Sonata* (1957), a film that is more notable for its art-star cast than for its formal experimentation.

Meanwhile, surrealism made a small comeback in Paris, thanks to filmmakers such as Ado Kyrou, Marcel Mariën, and Robert Benayoun—the latter took over the film magazine *Positif* in 1962. Yet few of those filmmakers managed to bring a genuine bite back into the genre, and few composed their films via automatism or other psychological techniques. Instead the surrealism of the 1960s and 1970s tended to embrace the more superficial side of the movement—its exaggeration, strangeness, and black humor—while introducing metaphysics and, in some cases, feminist theory. Alejandro Jodorowsky (*El Topo*, 1970), Fernando Arrabal (*Viva la muerte*, 1970), and Nelly Kaplan (*La fiancée du pirate*, 1969) made formally provocative films that were often labeled surreal for their ability to echo intense mind states, yet in truth they tended to favor imagery and symbolism over serious formal experimentation. Buñuel remained the exception, however. After returning to France for the first time in years he began to direct a series of intelligent, humorous, and subversive attacks on the bourgeoisie, including *Le Fantôme de la liberté* (*The Phantom of Liberty*, 1974) and *Cet obscur objet du désir* (*That Obscure Object of Desire*, 1977).

Hybrids also surfaced in Eastern Europe, Latin America, and Spain around the same time, and they too used a surrealist model to explore the mind and its deepest recesses. Yet for them, the embrace of the imagination had specific political implications, since the imagination was seen as a crucial antidote to both spiritual and political decay. "Surrealism offers a journey into the depths of the soul," said the Prague-based Jan Švankmajer, who was the most vocal proponent of the genre. And indeed, he and his contemporaries, who include Jiří Trnka, Karel Zeman, Pavel Juráček, Walerian Borowczyk, Juraj Jakubisko, and Dušan Makavejev, went on to create a number of spectacular and inventive films during the 1970s. Makavejev's *W.R.: Misterije organizma* (*W.R.: Mysteries of the Organism*, 1971) blends a heady mix of philosophical ideas, sexual frankness, and overt allegory into what Amos Vogel calls "unquestionably one of the most important subversive masterpieces of the 1970s." Yet it refuses to operate through typical narrative devices. "I believe I have been fighting narrative for years because narrative structure is a prison," said the director. "It is tradition; it is a lie; it is a formula that is imposed. But then I discovered that whatever I do, however I scramble my stories, not only do they have a beginning, middle, and end, but they each have their own shape. So I discovered that there is something indestructible in the story."

24

THIS PAGE AND OPPOSITE
Stills from 'The Blood of a Poet'
('Le Sang d'un poète', 1930)
Artist Jean Cocteau's first feature-length film
follows the hallucinatory life of a poet who gets
lost in his own creativity. While clearly the result
of Cocteau's interest in the subconscious,
the ambiguity of the film was often labeled
surrealist, but its concrete autobiographical
references and literal symbols tended to push
it into the realm of the cine-poem.

> *"Everything that emerges from the mind, even without logical form, inevitably reveals the singularity of that mind."*

Jean Goudal

TOP
Still from '8 x 8' (1957)
After emigrating to the United States to avoid prosecution in his native Germany, Hans Richter produced a number of surrealist films, which often had significant budgets, yet rarely explored the kind of provocation that defined his earlier works. For this film he used the game of chess to devise individual scenarios, or "moves," that featured his artist friends such as Marcel Duchamp, Max Ernst, Jean Arp, Alexander Calder, and Paul Bowles.

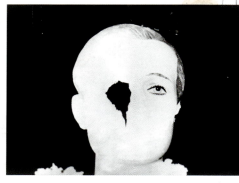

ABOVE
Still from 'Dom' (1958)
As the final collaborative film of the Polish graphic designers Jan Lenica and Walerian Borowczyk, this cut-out animation film concerning a common house retains Lenica's supreme craftsmanship and Borowczyk's dark sensibilities. It includes a number of surrealist moments, including a woman's wig running amok.

If the 1980s witnessed a decline in surrealist film, it was only because new theories of deconstruction, semiotics, and the simulacrum marshaled in a new era of theoretical engagement with the image. Thus the questioning of the mind took a backseat to the questioning of form, for example. The Chilean director Raúl Ruiz often imbued his features with an overt self-reflexive quality, which laid bare the fictional aspects of both his story lines and his characters. His *Trois vies et une seule mort* (*Three Lives and Only One Death*, 1996) follows the same actor, Marcello Mastroianni, as he leads multiple lives. But at the midpoint Ruiz undermines our trust of narrative and begins to intertwine Mastroianni's identities to the point where he begins to inhabit the "wrong" characters at the wrong time.

At this point, the metafictional aspect of surrealism falls in line with the neobaroque, where themes, images, and styles are cherry-picked from history and blended into a postmodern bricolage. As Michael Goddard observes, "the crucial difference between the baroque, as Ruiz understands it, and the ethos of cinematic surrealism, is the replacement of the motto, everything is fundamentally simple, with its opposite, everything is fundamentally complex."

That could also describe the cinema of David Lynch, which often confounds traditional notions of surrealism with a deep interest in abstract expressionism and complex psychological models. Since the early 1980s, Lynch has routinely filled his films with unexpected, often disturbing images that escape easy, linguistic definitions. In the process, he has repeatedly subverted the lives of his average, middle-class characters—from the suburban family of *Blue Velvet* (1986) to the blue-collar characters of *Inland Empire* (2006)—by pitting them against parallel worlds of darkness. This second or "third place," as Lynch titled one of his short films, is not only the world of the imagination, where normalcy disappears and irrationality begins, but a formalist strategy that deliberately emphasizes the plastic nature of cinema itself.

"The best for me," said Lynch, who puts more stock in daydreams than in dreaming, "is to combine the surface of a single story with the sensation of a dream, with the abstraction possible in a dream."

Lynch embraces another key aesthetic value of the surrealist approach, which has been consistent with virtually every generation: the aesthetic of visual clarity. Surrealism, after all, might be a deeply subjective practice, but by definition it is also a hyperrealist one. In its initial incarnation it denied the overblown, gestural quality of expressionism and favored instead the unmanipulated appearance of the everyday. That was very much in keeping with Franz Kafka's allegorical approach to literature, where the fantastic and the absurd are rendered in clear, precise prose. Even Alfred Hitchcock, who routinely trafficked in visual trickery, claimed that he "needed" Salvador Dalí to compose the dream sequence in *Spellbound* (1945) because he wanted someone who could "convey the dream with great visual sharpness and clarity—sharper than film itself."

That same idea can be found in a number of recent experimental film and video works, including the quiet, contemplative videos of Japan's Hiraki Sawa. His *Dwelling* (2002–2004) transforms a small London flat into a busy airport, with dozens of miniature passenger jets soaring through rooms, landing on countertops, and taxiing down hallways. Similarly, Belgium's Nicolas Provost, Sweden's Roy Andersson, and the American-Swiss duo Teresa Hubbard and Alexander Birchler shoot strangely unsettling scenes of everyday occurrences in exquisitely precise detail. "If there's a connection with the Belgian surrealist tradition with me,"

Stills from 'Faust' (1994)
Czechoslovakia's premier surrealist, Jan Švankmajer, took on the Faust myth by transforming the protagonist into a blue-collar worker whose life is transformed after he enters a dark puppet theater. There Švankmajer pulls out the stops to fuse fiction and reality, stop motion and live action, to paint a disturbing portrait of fear.

WATCH!
(and read Faust)

"Whatever comes out of my subconscious I use because I consider it to be the purest form. Everything else in your conscious being has been influenced by reality, art, education, your upbringing … But the original experiences that exist within you are the least corrupted of all."

Jan Švankmajer

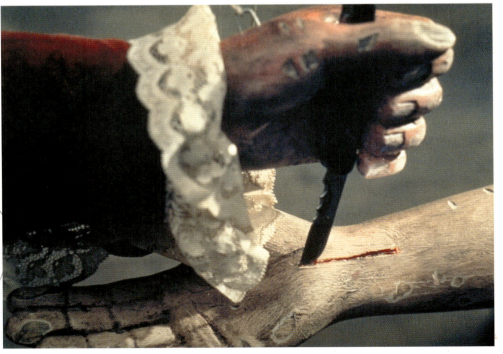

! subconscious thoughts are the purest ones!

Still from 'J'irai comme un cheval fou' (1973)
Arrabal's film compounds surrealist visions with black humor to tell the story of a young man's journey through the desert.

Still from 'Viva la muerte' (1970)
As a former member of Spain's anarchic Panic theater group, the Paris-based Fernando Arrabal defined his own filmmaking in opposition to surrealism. Yet his oedipal tale of a young boy searching for his abducted parents is chock-full of unexpected shocks, sexual provocation, and outright absurdity. In this scene the director makes a direct reference to the Viennese Actionists.

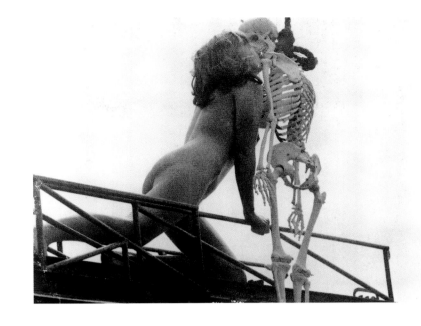

explains the Belgium-based Provost, "it's more to do with the quest for the common unconscious. I just try to surprise and fascinate the viewer as much as I can … trusting the viewer's common memory and then leaving the mystery unsolved."

Spike Jonze, Michel Gondry, Charlie Kaufman, Apichatpong Weerasethakul, Tony Oursler, Marnie Weber, Abigail Lane, Anthony Goicolea, Paulette Phillips, Janice Findley, and Ugo Rondinone continue the tradition in both cinematic and contemporary-art circles today.

Caribbean Pirates/Pirate Party (2001–2005)

If surrealism can be described as an attempt to de-sublimate subconscious urges and "transform the internal into a profound form of self-portraiture," as Susan M. Anderson writes, then the sculptor and performance artist Paul McCarthy can be viewed in a surrealist light.

For the better part of 30 years, he has made some of the most beguiling and often disturbing videos and installation artworks in the history of contemporary art. His *Sailor's Meat—Sailor's Delight* (1975) featured the artist in nothing more than a woman's blonde wig and blue eye shadow, carrying out a series of random, unrehearsed, psychosexual actions: He dons black lingerie, smears his body with ketchup, gags himself with a sausage, simulates intercourse with a pile of meat, and walks on broken glass.

For McCarthy, these performances—which often involve a never-ending flow of mock bodily fluids, including ketchup, mayonnaise, mustard, butter, chocolate, and motor oil—are an attempt to render both his body and the attendant space into expressionistic abstractions. Yet for audiences, his mumbling, unrepressed characters (which are deliberate parodies of pop-cultural icons including Popeye, Miss Piggy, and Pinocchio) can also be strangely affecting. As critic Linda Burnham remarked after seeing a performance in the 1970s, "The audience was trapped in a meditation with a madman."

Caribbean Pirates/Pirate Party (2001–2005) was made in collaboration with his son Damon, and it involves a large-scale movie set built in a studio in Baldwin Park, California. Here McCarthy takes on the role of a first mate whose sole job is to organize the ambush of a small island village. But for 90 minutes, characters wander in and out of the ship without rhyme or reason, stripping off their clothing, mumbling, yelling, playing with themselves, climbing through holes, smothering themselves in (fake) blood and feces, sodomizing their victims, cutting off limbs, attacking each other with machetes, and the like.

None of it makes any sense, of course, but none of it is supposed to. Instead, the viewer can only step back and understand the entire sloppy affair as a continuation of McCarthy's aesthetic, which is 1) a reflection of his interest in Viennese Aktionism, abstract expressionism, self-portraiture, the carnivalesque, and unrepressed, subconscious urges, and 2) a sardonic look at the way Hollywood structures reality through hackneyed story lines, characters, and distractions.

ABOVE
Still from 'Yellow Mellow' (2002)
For this video, the Belgian artist Nicolas Provost follows a lovesick figure as he dons a lion costume and wanders various cityscapes at night. No words are spoken and Provost's technique avoids linear storytelling, which leads to a sense of the uncanny.

OPPOSITE TOP
Still from 'The Floating House' (2002)
For this video installation, Canadian contemporary artist Paulette Phillips shot a single image of a 19th-Century house slowly sinking off the coast of Nova Scotia. While not a surrealist work, its dreamlike effect and strange incongruity give the film surrealist undertones.

OPPOSITE BOTTOM
Stills from 'Songs from the Second Floor' ('Sånger från andra våningen', 2000)
While composed of utterly bizarre, surreal moments that defy easy interpretations, this film by Sweden's Roy Andersson remains a cohesive, if not improbable, study of urban life.

"When I create my film I want to be sure that it will be, from one end to the other, a succession of wonders, because there is no point in bothering to see works that are not sensational."

Salvador Dalí

31

Still from 'The Ghost Trees' (2002)
California artist Marnie Weber uses homemade
sets and costumes to create stylized, ambiguous
fantasies that draw from children's tales as much
as from a surrealist penchant for the unexpected.

"I wanted to address consciousness,
subconsciousness, and superconsciousness —
that is a surrealistic consciousness where you
can comprehend the universe. For me film is
a metaphysical search."

Alejandro Jodorowsky

ABOVE
Still from 'Up in the Sky' (1997)
Australia's Tracey Moffatt is known for her highly stylized films, such as *Bedevil* (1993), which trade conventional narrative techniques for a more associative approach. Here she assembles 25 photographs that have no discernible relationship to one another, and yet are redolent of narrative suggestions. This allows viewers to invent scenarios of their own.

LEFT
Still from 'Dwelling' (2002)
Using software programs, the Japanese-born, London-based Hiraki Sawa transforms an ordinary flat into a bustling international airport by fusing original footage of passenger jets with his own dwelling.

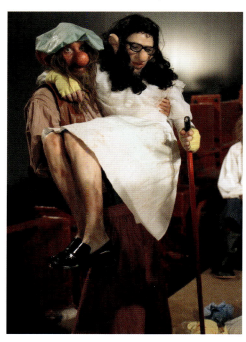

THIS PAGE AND OPPOSITE
**Stills from 'Caribbean Pirates/Pirate Party'
(2001–2005)**
Artist Paul McCarthy made a name for himself in
the 1970s with his brash performance-art pieces,
which seemed to channel unconscious urges
and a pop-art version of Viennese Actionism.
During that period he began using common
fluids in place of bodily fluids, such as ketchup
for blood or chocolate for feces. But with this
feature-length film, he and his son, Damon,
take that idea to the extreme. Here they work
with a full-scale pirate frigate and dozens of
masked marauders who attack their victims
without mercy, including a pair that seem to
be channeling the husband and wife from
Who's Afraid of Virginia Woolf?.

Post-Surrealism and the Mythopoeic

[handwritten: bring Jungian Psychology alongside Freudian's 'Uncanny'?]

[handwritten: Jean Cocteau]

As surrealism made its way west in the 1930s and 1940s, it collided with a new era of change in America. That is when perception and cognition were being challenged by a revolution in the social sciences, which went hand in hand with the birth of a new middle class. As a result, the period saw a new wave of experimentation in the arts, which ultimately led to abstract expressionism, improvisation, conceptualism, and post-surrealist collage.

While utterly diverse, these movements were united by an ever-deepening interest in Jungian psychology, Zen Buddhism, esoteric knowledge, and a more life-affirming inner experience. This was an era when the poem and the novel generally replaced music as an organizational principle for experimental filmmakers, and deliberate messages replaced the surrealist idea of the irrational. As P. Adams Sitney observes, underground filmmakers began to use "elaborate mythic structures that equated the dialectics of individual consciousness, with the lamentable struggles of gods, demigods, much as the romantic poets, William Blake, Percy Bysshe Shelley, Friedrich Hölderlin, and Victor Hugo had done."

Thus one can see an almost palpable romanticism in the mythopoeic films of the late 1940s and 1950s, in particular those by the Americans Harry Smith, Curtis Harrington, Gregory J. Markopoulos, Ed Emshwiller, Kenneth Anger, and, to a lesser extent, Maya Deren and Sara Arledge. These filmmakers generally saw themselves working in a tradition of cine-poetics as defined by European filmmakers such as Jean Epstein, Germaine Dulac, Robert Wiene, Luis Buñuel, and Jean Cocteau. "Buñuel and Cocteau were gods to us," explains filmmaker Curtis Harrington. "We wanted to make dream films, which were the antithesis of commercial films. We wanted to use film as a purely creative, intensely personal act."

Indeed, these filmmakers were part of a new generation of film artists who used film as their only medium, as opposed to using it to augment their painterly or sculptural practices. And like the dreamy, mythical films of Cocteau, namely *La belle et la bête* (*Beauty and the Beast*, 1946) and *Orphée* (1950), they used mythic sources to explore deeply personal themes. Markopoulos, in particular, used mythological subject matter throughout his career, yet developed his own highly individualistic visual language. Indeed, his films, which include *Swain* (1950), *Twice a Man* (1963), *Eros, O Basileus* (1967), *The Mysteries* (1968), and the monumental *Eniaios* (1948–1990), which comprises over 100 short films culled from the

Still from 'Beauty and the Beast' ('La belle et la bête', 1946)
France's Jean Cocteau combined his own interest in the subconscious with an updated version of Jeanne-Marie le Prince de Beaumont's fairy tale to create a moving portrait of unrequited love.

"One must use a brazen lie to convince people of a reality of a higher and deeper order."
Jean Cocteau

"[I am for] the use of short film phrases which evoke thought images."

Gregory Markopoulos

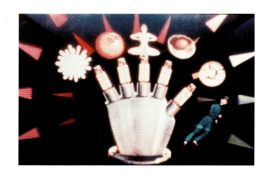

ABOVE AND TOP
Stills from 'Number 10 and 11: Mirror Animations'
(1957–1962)
Drawing from Buddhism, the kabbalah, alchemy, and other mystical symbols, Harry Smith's classic animated collage film is a study of the jazz great Thelonious Monk and his *Mysterioso*.

filmmaker's entire career, are haunted works, where figures appear and disappear in a gentle flow, sometimes moving the story forward, sometimes backward. If they share a common idea, it is a central concern with the nature of desire and all its manifestations. *The Illiac Passion* (1967), in particular, achieves its effects through both a meticulous use of montage techniques and formal aesthetic values drawn from Renaissance paintings—namely the use of Euclidean composition, tableaux, and vivid colors. What is more, he reintroduced the idea of the fade-out in particularly affecting ways. As P. Adams Sitney has observed: "Fading in and out may be interpreted as a psychological distancing or phrasing of the images as in remote memory."

Harry Smith brought an even more aggressive mythopoesis to his handmade collage animations of the same period. His *Number 10 and 11: Mirror Animations* (1957–1962) owe an obvious debt to both Max Ernst and Raymond Roussel in their free use of mythical figures and strange, nonsensical fairy-tale constructions. *Number 11* follows the exploits of a letter carrier trying to deliver a note to his beloved. In the process, he encounters objects and characters that magically transform—snowflakes expand into the kabbalistic Tree of Life, a bird transforms into a human skull, and human heads transform into eyeballs. "These films describe analogies among tarot cards, kabbalistic symbolism, Indian chiromancy and dancing, Buddhist mandalas, and Renaissance alchemy," said Smith, who was allegedly consecrated as a gnostic bishop in the Ecclesia Gnostica Catholica. "But you shouldn't be looking at this as a continuity. Film frames are hieroglyphs, even when they look like actuality. You should think of the individual frame, always as a glyph, and then you'll understand what cinema is all about."

That idea finds a fuller realization in the films of Kenneth Anger, who often employed a darker, more subversive agenda. Like Smith's, his films are rife with hexagrams, triangles, tattoos, pagan deities, tarot cards, planetary references, and a color palette drawn from Aleister Crowley's *Magick* (1912). But unlike Smith, Anger

ABOVE AND RIGHT
Stills from 'Sunstone' (1979)
The pioneer video artist Ed Emshwiller routinely explored human nature's relationship to the cosmos and the self. Here he uses the sun as a Georges Méliès–style filmmaker who seems to enable consciousness.

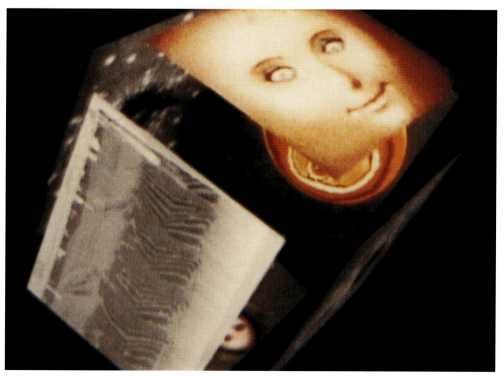

"For those who are interested [in my films], numbers 1–5 were made under pot, number 6 with schmek and ups, number 7 with cocaine and ups, numbers 8–12 with almost anything but mainly deprivation, and number 13 with green pills from Max Johnson and pink pills from Tim Leary."

Harry Smith

Still from 'Relativity' (1966)
Using themes of physicality, sexuality, and death, Emshwiller's highly seductive 16mm film attempts to make a connection between the emotions and our perception of the environment.

believed that symbols—whether filmed or encountered in real life—could manifest the occult when combined with a person's will. As author Anna Powell explains, "He regards film as having the potential, when properly used, to invoke primal forces, perhaps even demons. Once released, these demons can affect not only those involved in the film's production, but also, through a series of occult circuits connecting physical with spiritual dimensions of existence, the film's audience."

More importantly, he combines such incantatory images with pop-cultural references and pop-music cues to "speak directly to the baser (and darker) side of the human psyche," as Bruce Jenkins describes his work. His third version of *Inauguration of the Pleasure Dome* (1954–1966), which was displayed on three screens, features archetypal satyrs and witches indulging in celebrations and orgies. Similarly, *Scorpio Rising* (1963) finds its tension in the contrast between enduring myths of cowboys and bikers, fascism, Christianity, and Hollywood; and *Lucifer Rising* (1970–1981) uses the holy war between the Piscean age and the Aquarian as the jumping-off point for a spellbinding meditation on polytheism.

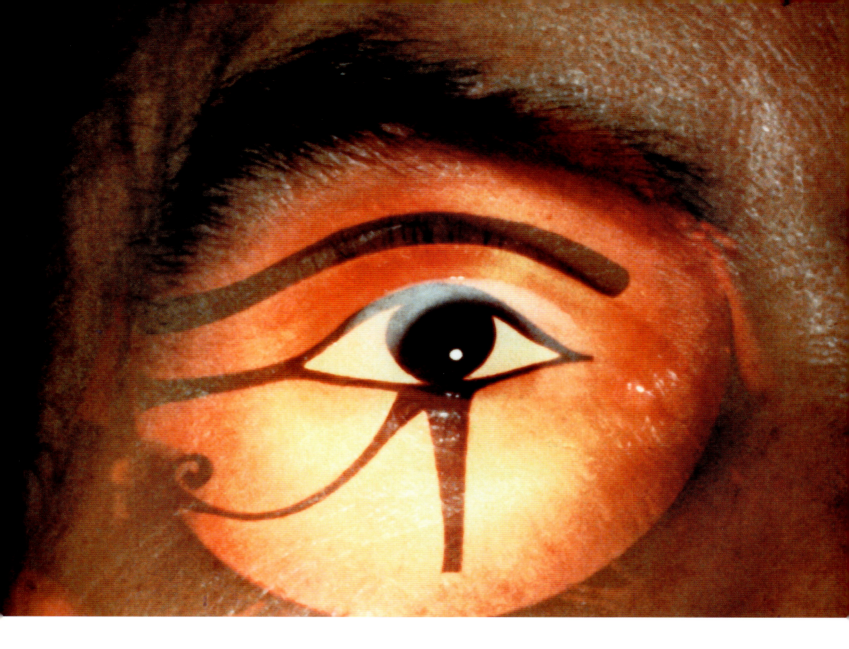

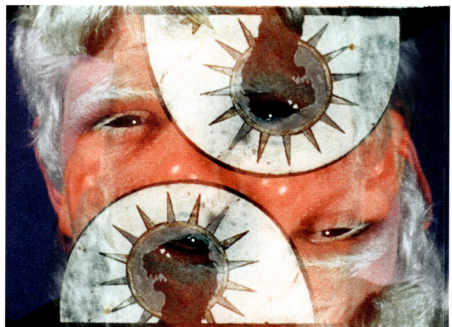

THIS PAGE AND OPPOSITE
Stills from 'Inauguration of the Pleasure Dome' (1954–1966)
Existing in numerous versions, including at least one with multiple screens, Kenneth Anger's most celebrated work portrays a Black Mass at the house of Shiva, which quickly becomes a party attended by an array of mythical figures. In the process Anger blends pop-cultural icons with hermetic, black-magic themes, astrological symbols, and images from esoteric traditions.

"Making a movie is casting a spell."
Kenneth Anger

"Metaphor is the most outstanding of all the various elements of rhetoric."

Pier Paolo Pasolini

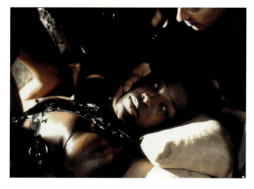

TOP
Still from 'The Long Road to Mazatlan' (1999)
The London-based artist Isaac Julien is known for his multiple-screen, stylized videos that use intense, kaleidoscopic colors, costumes, and sets. Here he combines Western motifs with direct cinematic references from Martin Scorsese, Andy Warhol, and David Hockney to create an oblique reference to race relations and sexual mores in contemporary society.

ABOVE
Still from 'The Attendant' (1993)
Here Isaac Julien uses the story of a museum guard confronting his own repressed desires to further explore expressive visual motifs. As the guard falls under the spell of individual paintings, this multichannel work explodes into a kaleidoscope of high-gloss, ecstatic moments, from Busby Berkeley–esque dance numbers to theatrical S-M scenes.

If there is a marked decadence to these films, it clearly corresponds to the symbolist's obsession with death, sexual ambiguity, and an intensification of sensual input. Of course, esoteric scholarship and mythology were very much a part of the 1960s and 1970s counterculture movement, which in turn influenced mainstream cinema, with Federico Fellini delving into *Satyricon* (1969), Miklós Jancsó shooting *Szerelmem, Elektra* (*Electra, My Love*, 1974), and Alejandro Jodorowsky mounting his staggering epic, *The Holy Mountain* (1973). Pier Paolo Pasolini, in particular, devoted himself almost exclusively to mythopoeic themes in the late 1960s and 1970s. His films *Edipo re* (*Oedipus Rex*, 1967), *Teorema* (*Theorem*, 1968), and *Il Decameron* (*The Decameron*, 1971) are peopled with contemporary figures—from beggars to priests, prostitutes to aristocrats—acting out ancient story lines culled from the mythological canon. Yet, as he said of *Edipo re*, "instead of trying to reconcile the myth with modern psychology, I took the Oedipus complex and projected it back into myth."

Nevertheless, the mythopoeic genre lost some footing in the 1970s, at least among experimental filmmakers and contemporary artists, primarily due to the popularity of both minimalism and conceptualism, which began to offer serious challenges to the "decorative" sensibilities of mythic narratives. At this time a number of influential artists began to drain the meaning from their images rather than pile on reference upon reference. Some filmmakers found a balance, however, including Ed Emshwiller, James Broughton, David Lebrun, and Ian Hugo. The latter's *Reborn* (1979) uses superimposition and basic camera tricks to create a magical atmosphere imbued by floating characters and mythical overtones, including a Madonna-like spirit (played by Anaïs Nin) who advises the protagonist to cast aside his mocking shadow in order to survive.

Mythopoeic themes have been more recently embraced by a number of contemporary artists, including Germany's Werner Nekes (*Uliisses*, 1982), the UK's Isaac Julien (*The Attendant*, 1993), Hungary's Béla Tarr (*Werckmeister Harmonies*, 2000), and America's Matthew Barney (*The Cremaster Cycle*, 1995–2002), although often to different ends.

Barney, in particular, offers a heady mix of mythology, pop culture, autobiography, and the filmmaker's personal obsessions over a span of five feature-length films and videos. Yet, at its core, *The Cremaster Cycle* remains true to one basic idea: the body's manifestation of gender (the cremaster is the muscle that lowers and raises the testicles). Thus, as each film explores a different mythical scenario, from the building of the Chrysler Building by Masons to the execution of Gary Gilmore, it continually refers back to the theme of physiological evolution. The floating blimps in *Cremaster 1* have obvious symbolic value, as does the sexual union with a queen bee in *Cremaster 2*, the construction of the very phallic Chrysler Building in *Cremaster 3*, the actual manifestation of the testes in *Cremaster 4*, and the magician's transcendence/death in *Cremaster 5*.

Yet Barney eschews traditional storytelling and opts instead for an associative, almost surrealist methodology—often without dialogue or plot development. In fact it might be interesting to compare his work to the "silent" operas of Robert Wilson, where seemingly random symbols are woven into a tapestry of rich tableaux vivants. After all, both artists prefer to have their work affect the viewer on a subconscious, as opposed to a conscious, level. And both artists tend to use mythic subjects in a more painterly way, where they are emptied, manipulated, and personalized. As Barney says, his move into cinema came only after realizing that sculpture was "too limited" by both stasis and gravity. So he turned to film to give his sculptural creations—which are both characters and props in his film—a life and a history, which in turn follows them into the gallery. "The forms don't really take on life for me," said Barney, "until they've been 'eaten,' passed through the narrative construction."

The Holy Mountain (1973)

Alejandro Jodorowsky's *The Holy Mountain* represents a fascinating confluence of ideas, trends, and movements that were popular in the late 1960s and early 1970s. Namely: countercultural idealism, mythopoeic aesthetics, political allegory, and new-age metaphysics.

Produced by Beatles manager Allen Klein, who initially brought in John Lennon and George Harrison as financial backers, the film owes its structure to a number of specific sources, including *The Divine Comedy* (1308–1321) by Dante, *The Ascent of Mount Carmel* (1578–1579) by St. John of the Cross, and, less directly, *La hora de los hornos* (*The Hour of the Furnaces*, 1968) by Fernando Solanas. It is, nonetheless, a wholly original film that follows the unlikely adventures of a lowly thief who first bears witness to the exploitation of an unnamed South American country by capitalists, and then joins some of those same capitalists on a quest to find eternal life.

Such plot descriptions fail to convey the true strength of the film, however, which delights in a wicked Buñuelian black humor and an array of genuinely striking images. During the first section, which is rendered without dialogue, the thief bears witness to a number of disturbing events, including the massacre of civilians by peacekeeping soldiers, a drunken night with Romans who end up producing the thief's beatific image on thousands of crucifixes, and a circus sideshow that recreates the bloody invasion of South America by Spanish conquistadors—with costumed cane toads. "You can call the picture surrealist if you want to," explains Jodorowsky. "But only because it is not realist. It is ridiculous to call any film realistic, because it is *not* real. It cannot be!"

Indeed, the second section of the film becomes even more absurdist as Jodorowsky introduces a number of characters, including a female weapons manufacturer, a political adviser, a cynical pop artist, a chief of police, and a designer of war toys. These characters, each more conceited than the next, have been summoned by a master alchemist, played by Jodorowsky, who promises to teach them the secret of immortality. During this stage of the film Jodorowsky uses elaborate staging reminiscent of Ken Russell, with vivid colors, exacting compositions, and iconic characters based on the tarot. "At the time I wanted to make holy pictures," recalls Jodorowsky. "Pictures that could change the public."

He also wanted to change himself. As he says, he sought the help of a real shaman, Oscar Ichazo of the Arica Institute, and hired him as a spiritual guide. And according to Jodorowsky, Ichazo put him through a series of rituals and tests over several weeks, which included the use of both LSD and marijuana and a hefty fee of $17,000. "At the time I was obsessed with reaching enlightenment," said the director, who is now an authority on the tarot, world mythology, and Eastern metaphysics. "So I thought that the film could be as sacred as an initiation, or a holy book, and we had to *live* it."

PAGES 46 & 47
Stills from 'Cremaster 3' (2002)
Artist Matthew Barney's five-cycle project uses specific mythical, personal, and pop-cultural references to create dreamlike narratives that verge on the abstract.

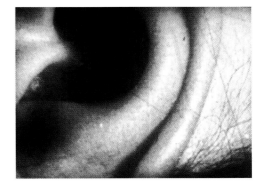

TOP
Still from 'Geography of the Body' (1943)
With commentary by the poet George Parker, filmmaker Willard Maas uses extreme magnification of the human figure to hint at the exploration of undiscovered continents.

ABOVE
Still from 'Fragment of Seeking' (1946)
Made while he was a student, Curtis Harrington's portrait of the adolescent Narcissus uses experimental techniques of temporal manipulations and spatial contrasts.

> "I see films as a research tool that comes out of mythology."
>
> Alejandro Jodorowsky

ABOVE
Production still from 'The Holy Mountain' (1973)
Alejandro Jodorowsky directing.

LEFT
Still from 'The Holy Mountain' (1973)
As the film comes to a close, Jodorowsky shifts into a neorealist style as the alchemist exposes the falsehood of representation—including that of the film itself—to the capitalists.

MIDDLE
Still from 'The Holy Mountain' (1973)
The capitalists are tested again by the alchemist.

BOTTOM
Still from 'The Holy Mountain' (1973)
Using elaborate sets reminiscent of Ken Russell, Jodorowsky gathers the capitalists for the first time and asks them to dispense with their monetary possessions.

OPPOSITE TOP
Still from 'The Holy Mountain' (1973)
Alejandro Jodorowsky's epic follows two characters: a fool who gets mistaken for Jesus and an alchemist who leads a group of capitalists on a journey of self-discovery. In this scene the fool approaches the inner sanctum of the alchemist.

OPPOSITE MIDDLE
Still from 'The Holy Mountain' (1973)
Using the kind of precise framing that recalls Stanley Kubrick, Jodorowsky, as the alchemist, cleanses and shaves the heads of two initiates.

OPPOSITE BOTTOM
Still from 'The Holy Mountain' (1973)
After a drunken night, the fool is kidnapped by entrepreneurs, who quickly recreate his likeness to sell to the masses.

Abstraction and the Lyrical Film

Abstract cinema has been around for nearly 100 years, yet it remains one of the most difficult genres for general audiences to understand, simply because of its nonrepresentational form. It is, after all, the absolute antithesis of commercial narrative cinema. But it can also be one of the richest, if not the most sophisticated, subgenres of experimental filmmaking.

The aesthetic has its roots in abstract painting, which emerged in artistic circles over a century ago. At the time, artists were beginning to realize that representational painting had reached an impasse—that it could no longer "reveal the invisible" as it once did, or make profound statements about the modern world as it did during the Renaissance. Instead artists began to look to the cinema as a tool to explore ideas culled from such artistic movements as futurism, Dada, constructivism, suprematism, cubism, and even Rimbaud's drunken symbolist synesthesia. These experiments took place simultaneously with the growth of narrative cinema, yet offered distinctly different results.

Some of the earliest experiments in this area occurred with painting directly onto celluloid, otherwise known as the camera-less film. New Zealand's Len Lye deserves special attention here, not only for being a pioneer, but for creating some of the first genuine masterpieces of the genre, including *Tusalava* (1929), *A Color Box* (1935), and *Trade Tattoo* (1937). Since then, the camera-less film has become an entire subgenre unto itself, with its own vocabulary and techniques. There are, for example, the jazzy, hand-painted abstractions of Harry Smith, Marie Menken, Stan Brakhage, and José Antonio Sistiaga, which explode with bombastic bursts of energy and color. Conversely, filmmakers such as Jürgen Reble, Ties Poeth, William Raban, and Luis Recoder tend to expose raw celluloid to chemical baths—both organic and artificial—to create mesmerizing patterns of staggering complexity.

But the true flowering of abstract cinema came in the 1920s, both in France and Germany. That is when a number of artists/filmmakers began to search for an abstract visual language that could speak directly to the senses—much like a painting. The Russian-born, German-based painter Wassily Kandinsky was just one of many who drew a direct corollary between painterly elements (colors, shapes, and forms) and musical qualities (tonal scales, volume, and harmonies). "Sound is the soul of form," wrote Kandinsky. "And form is the outer expression of the inner content."

TOP AND ABOVE
Stills from 'Rainbow Dance' (1936)
New Zealand's pioneer experimental filmmaker, Len Lye, used hand-painting techniques and Technicolor film to create vivid, painterly works that the artist described as "pure figures of motion painting."

OPPOSITE
Film strips from 'Death of the Gorilla' (1965–66)
Mirroring the media-obsessed mind-set of the 1960s, Peter Mays created this hypnotic film by shooting scenes off a television set and transforming them into a dense, layered collage.

Still from 'Light Rhythms' (1930)
Another lyrical study of light movement by Francis Bruguière and collaborator Oswell Blakeston, where tonal shifts playing across sculptures are used to render the picture plane ambiguous.

Coincidentally, abstract cinema grew along parallel lines, where "visual music" could be created out of animated shapes, lines, and forms. Germany's Walter Ruttmann, the Germany-based Viking Eggeling, and Hans Richter were three of the genre's most important pioneers, and they each had a distinct visual style. Richter came close to finding a visual corollary to Johann Sebastian Bach's sonatas in his films *Rhythmus 23* (1923) and *Rhythmus 25* (1925), and Ruttmann's *Opus* films (1921–1925) were buoyant, lyrical renditions of pure line and color. Yet it was Germany's Oskar Fischinger who ultimately became known as the genre's most popular technician. Inspired by Ruttmann's painstakingly hand-colored *Lichtspiel: Opus 1* (1921), as well as his own interest in color, music, science, and spirituality, he made 12 *Studies* between 1929 and 1932 that were often shown in large concert halls with live musical accompaniment. With these films Fischinger achieved a genuine symbiosis between classical and pop music cues and animated graphics, where dancing lines, shapes, and forms performed very much like tones, rhythms, and harmonies.

Fischinger's sphere of influence expanded after he moved to Los Angeles in the late 1930s at the behest of director Ernst Lubitsch. There, through occasional screenings at museums (in particular San Francisco's legendary *Art in Cinema* show of 1947), his films inspired a new generation of abstract filmmakers, most notably John and James Whitney and Jordan Belson, who were developing their own visual languages. This new generation opted to move abstract cinema toward a more ephemeral and spiritual place, one that was more subjective and less inclined toward graphic representations. That was very much in keeping with what was going on in the fine arts at the time. The American post-surrealist group the Dynaton had begun to move painterly abstraction into a more spiritual realm, or what they called a "limitless continuum." Also, Fischinger had expressed interest in the meditative quality of Eastern devotional paintings, which were popular among artists of the early 1900s. But the Whitneys, Belson, and Thomas Wilfred were arguably the first to bring cinema closer to a wholly meditative cinema.

The first attempts of the Whitneys yielded abstract shapes through meticulous animation techniques, which were exceptionally innovative for their time. Their *Five Film Exercises* (1943–1944) was not only the first film to use a mechanical pendulum system to create its soundtrack (based on Arnold Schoenberg's dodecaphonic system), but remains one of the earliest films to use code as its basic language.

From there the Whitneys developed their own motion-control system through the use of a military computer tracking system, which enabled them to layer their work in minute increments. As a result they were able to create quiet, delicate compositions that would swim and morph into nebulous fields of color. James Whitney's *Lapis* (1966) was remarkable for its singular image—a slowly morphing mandala buzzing with millions of tiny, vibrating atoms. Whitney later claimed that the film, which has been hailed as one of the true masterpieces of abstract cinema by Kerry Brougher, was an attempt to "capture the wave patterns of the brain at rest." And that is just what it does. As Brougher writes, "with its continually quivering energy particles swimming in a cosmic void and magnetically attracted and repelled around a central mandala form, it seems to be on the brink of revealing some truth about the structure of the universe."

Thomas Wilfred went even further in dematerializing the image through a complex interplay of warped mirrors, beveled glass, and jewels. His Lumia experiments, as he called them, projected light in real time onto frosted glass. These were totally ephemeral images that seemed to exist in a liminal state that could run for days without repeating. Meanwhile, the Chicago-born, San Francisco-based Jordan Belson went on to perfect his own cinematic abstractions, where sweeping,

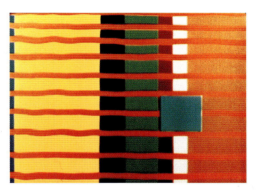

ABOVE
Still from 'Radio Dynamics' (1942)
Beginning his career in the Weimar Republic in the early 1920s, Fischinger's pioneering films in moving abstractions were greatly influenced by modernist theories on color, rhythm, and synesthesia. *Radio Dynamics*, which was created after his break with Walt Disney in California, is a silent film that uses slower, pulsating rhythms of colorful forms much like his paintings.

TOP
Still from 'Allegretto' (1936–1943)
German filmmaker Oskar Fischinger employs a painted-cell technique to great effect in this film, the first he made upon his arrival in the United States. Playful diamond shapes, zigzags, and Deco designs dance to the upbeat tempo of composer Ralph Rainger.

LEFT
Still from 'Film Study' (1925)
The detached eyeball is a common theme running throughout the history of experimental cinema. Here, Hans Richter serves up an early example, a lively mix of distortion mirrors and live action, which grew out of his roots in Dada.

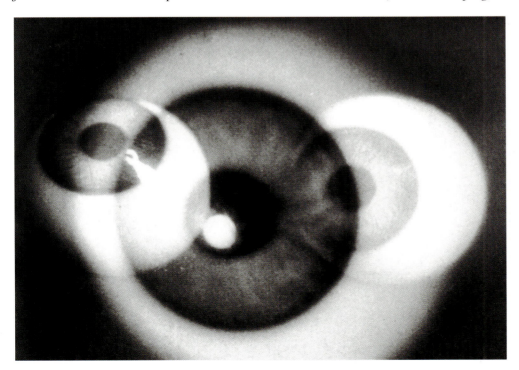

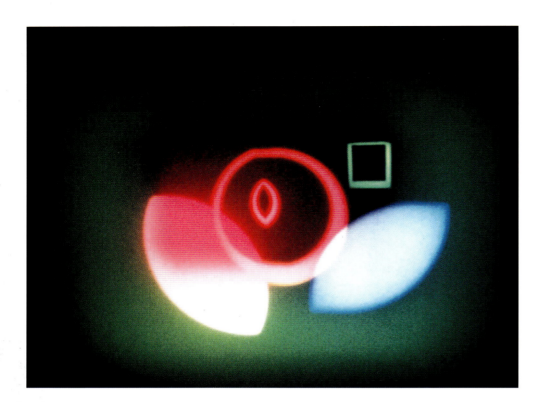

LEFT
Still from 'Five Film Exercises' (1943–44)
This is a key film in the advancement of the "visual music" genre, made by California's Whitney brothers during World War II. The original score was made through a complex pendulum system that could record directly onto the optical-track area of the film.

BELOW
Still from 'Arabesque' (1975)
Considered by many to be the father of computer animation, John Whitney made this meditative film featuring hand-drawn forms that quietly bloom and morph to music by the Persian classical composer Manoochehr Sadeghi.

have a look (as an inspiration for major project) !

ABOVE
Still from 'Lapis' (1966)
James Whitney's masterpiece took seven
years to complete using a mechanical analog
computer–controlled animation system. The
result is a singular image that appears to be
slowly pulsing, shifting, and rotating to a
calming score of sitar music.

LEFT
The Whitneys' studio (circa 1943)
This is where the Whitney brothers developed
their own equipment for composing sound and
animation for their abstract films.

majestic, overwhelming fields of ephemeral shapes and vivid colors were woven together into nebulous, gaseous clouds or galaxies.

Others of the same period found their own abstract methodologies. The painter James Davis modulated reflections and tonal hues (*Light Reflections*, 1948), Douglas Crockwell photographed oil on glass (*Glen Falls Sequence*, 1946), and Mary Ellen Bute created an array of complex models in her studio that transformed light into delicate shadow symphonies (*Rhythm in Light*, 1934). The work of Marie Menken, Dwinell Grant, and Alexandre Vitkine continued the tradition in the 1950s, and Storm de Hirsch, Gary Doberman, Carmen D'Avino, and many others followed suit in the 1960s.

The majority of these experiments were made on celluloid, both 16mm and 35mm, but by the late 1960s and 1970s a number of artists began to recognize the abstract potential of both analog video and digital effects. John Whitney Jr., Stan VanDerBeek, and Ed Emshwiller were early pioneers in that area, but as the medium began to dovetail with the burgeoning electronic-music scene in the mid- to late 1960s, a new generation of videographers emerged with the likes of Steve Beck, David Ehrlich, Ken Knowlton, Dan Sandin, Henry Flynt, and Steina and Woody Vasulka. For these artists, video synthesizers offered not only a way to create "a new form of constructivist abstraction," as Beck describes his own practice, but an attempt to stimulate the optic neural system directly. Beck applied "pulsed stimulation signals" directly to the eyelid in 1968 to "get away from the screen and the image completely," as he says, "and affect images directly from the body itself, much like phosphenes and other eidetic images."

More recently, with the advent of digital software, a new generation of "ambient" cinema has emerged, which tends to refer back to the more metaphysical approach of earlier pioneers such as Wilfred and Belson. Like those filmmakers, these ambient artists are looking to create seamless visual flows that continually morph into incandescent, spectral sculptures in real time. They include George Stadnik, Chris Casady, Jeffers Egan, Ian Helliwell, and Jun'ichi Okuyama.

Abstraction in general is defined by a desire to intensify subjectivity, which is at the heart of every expressionist's desire to go beyond realism, hackneyed scripts, or the limits of the imagination. Yet if anyone deserves credit for cresting the wave of a truly expressionistic cinema it is the American filmmaker Stan Brakhage. Born in 1933 in Kansas City, Missouri, Brakhage became a tireless promoter of the "personal film" in the 1950s and 1960s, and his innovation and theories ultimately changed the medium forever.

His real breakthrough came in the late 1950s, as he began to immerse himself more and more in his subjects. By the end of the decade he realized that he could free himself of dramatic structures altogether and use images—both figurative and abstract—in the manner of stanzas, or notes in a score. "That's when I grew as a film artist," he told an interviewer. "Once I did that I began to feel all history, all life, all that I would have as material with which to work, would have come from the inside of me rather than some form imposed from the outside in."

At this point cinema becomes a direct representation of the filmmaker's emotions and sensibilities. Brakhage's *Anticipation of the Night* (1958) is a haunting daydream of a film, where a childbirth morphs into the moon, a rose morphs into the sun, and the opening of a doorway becomes quite literally an opening of the subconscious. As filmmaker and Brakhage's longtime friend Phil Solomon says, "With that film he comes up with a new kind of first-person cinema, where you no longer need the

ABOVE
Mary Ellen Bute (circa 1953)
Pioneer animator Mary Ellen Bute worked from 1933 and had many of her abstract films projected at Radio City Music Hall.

TOP
Marie Menken (circa 1955)
Filmmaker and socialite Marie Menken in her studio, where she made her delicate, personal, abstract works.

OPPOSITE TOP
Still from 'Energies' (1957)
James Davis started exploring glass reflections in the 1940s, which he compared to both the "patterns of flowing energy" and the symbol for cosmogenesis.

OPPOSITE BOTTOM LEFT
Still from 'Come Closer' (1952)
America's Hy Hirsh was an essential figure in the history of abstract film. For this film he experimented in 3-D processes.

OPPOSITE BOTTOM RIGHT
Still from 'Gyromorphosis' (1956)
Hy Hirsh's film combines notions of abstract jazz, the theories of the Bauhaus, and the kinetic sculpture of the Dutch painter Constant Nieuwenhuis.

Still from 'Video Weavings' (1974)
Stephen Beck was a pioneer in flattening video's image and enhancing its plasticity through his own self-designed video synthesizers. Here his Beck Video Weaver enhances analog signals to create ever-changing patterns of color.

BELOW RIGHT
Still from 'Patterns of Interference' (2000)
The UK's Ian Helliwell is perhaps best known for his multiscreen 8mm film performances and light shows that use found footage, homemade collages, and moving filters. He also produces hand-painted 8mm films such as this one, which invokes an amateurish, lo-fi sensibility of great immediacy.

mediator—the actor—to carry the emotions. [This is where] you can do it directly, from thought to film; where the man behind the camera would now be the protagonist."

An intense subjectivity was, of course, at the heart of German expressionism in the early 1900s, most notably in the work of F. W. Murnau and Robert Wiene. By the 1930s filmmakers began to see a parallel between an intense cinematic subjectivity and consciousness itself. The Japanese filmmakers Teinosuke Kinugasa and Masao Inoue were arguably the first to see a parallel between filmic subjectivity and the Buddhist idea of a subject/object synthesis—where the seer and the seen are one and the same. But Brakhage went further than anyone in what would later become known as the lyrical genre, which is, for the most part, a purely stream-of-consciousness cinema defined completely by the filmmaker's subjectivity. Indeed, in *Window Water Baby Moving* (1959), *Dog Star Man* (1961–1964), and dozens of later works such as *Unconscious London Strata* (1982), he achieves a wholly introverted impressionism that is perhaps most remarkable for its expressive use of color.

But to define Brakhage's films in terms of imagery would be to deny what is probably most crucial to his aesthetic: rhythm and tempo. "Because if you pay real close attention to the work," explains Solomon, "the work invites you in and it actually does have a kind of mind's ear. You can hear every cut in a Brakhage film."

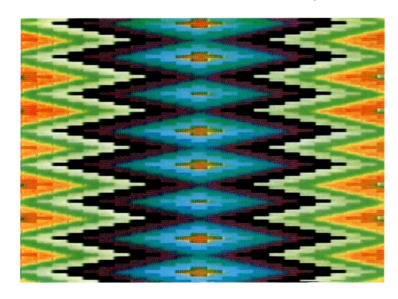

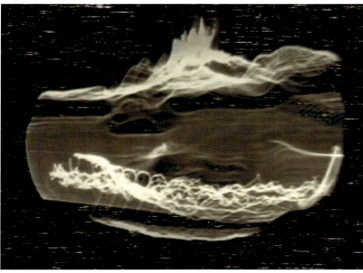

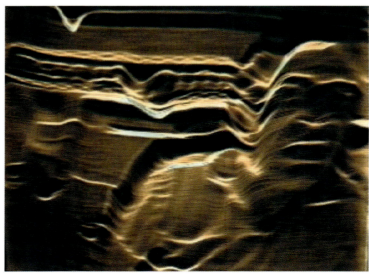

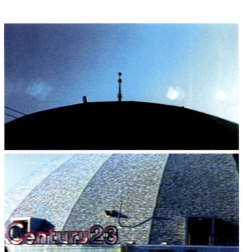

THIS PAGE
Stills from 'Winchester Redux' (2004)
New York's Jeremy Blake often used digital technologies and collage techniques to realize intensely subjective videos that verged on the psychedelic. His *Winchester Redux* was inspired by California's Sarah Winchester Mystery House of 1884, which is filled with hidden and haunted rooms. Thus this multichannel work becomes a metaphor for the mind.

OPPOSITE BOTTOM LEFT
Still from 'C-Trend' (1974)
Using a Rutt/Etra Scan Processor, Woody Vasulka breaks down another image in real time until it seems to reflect little more than the medium itself—a buzzing blur of electronic signals.

OPPOSITE BOTTOM RIGHT
Still from 'Telc' (1974)
Woody and Steina Vasulka are two crucial artists in the history of video art. Here Woody uses a video synthesizer to abstract a moving image to the point of making it a kind of a topological map, where colors and tones become a tapestry of moving peaks and valleys.

Lyricism also defines Bruce Baillie's empirical approach, which evolved from subjective documentaries in the early 1960s to a more abstract, impressionistic approach a short time later. His *Quick Billy* (1970) is a kind of impressionistic road film imbued with a steady stream of intense personal reflections. Here the filmmaker uses his own, prior diary notes, which were made directly, in the heat of the moment, as a guide for his camera. Thus notations such as "frightening brilliance, the sun, the ocean, the stars, the flame, the green jewels emanating rainbow" became a shooting

"For me video is less a tool for recording external reality than a way to show psychological and physiological inner worlds—like finding symbolic colors and speeds for different states of mind, or creating images that look like those graphic formations called afterimages that you see when you close your eyes."
Pipilotti Rist

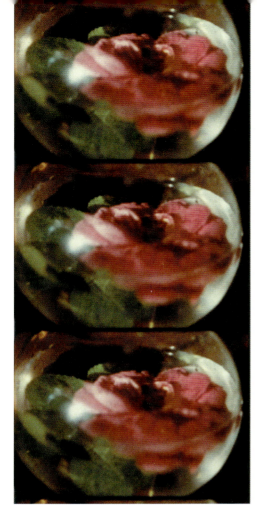

THIS PAGE
Film strips from 'Anticipation of the Night' (1958)
For Stan Brakhage, this 1958 film was a breakthrough in that it replaces a central protagonist with the camera's point of view. That allows the viewer to identify not with a character but with the camera itself.

OPPOSITE LEFT
Film strip from "existence is song" (1987)
Using 35mm and 70mm fragments, Stan Brakhage's abstract film *The Dante Quartet*, which includes this segment, was painstakingly composed over six years. The film's extraordinary array of luminous colors was the result of chemical washes, drips, and scratches, which were carefully modulated to find a visual tone comparable to Dante's text.

OPPOSITE CENTER
Film strip of 'Naughts' (1994)
More ephemeral and quiet than some of Brakhage's earlier works, this film features hand-painted effects grouped into distinct movements.

OPPOSITE RIGHT
Film strip from 'Stately Mansions Did Decree' (1999)
The flickering shards of red and orange in this spectacular hand-painted Brakhage film suggest a universe ablaze with energy.

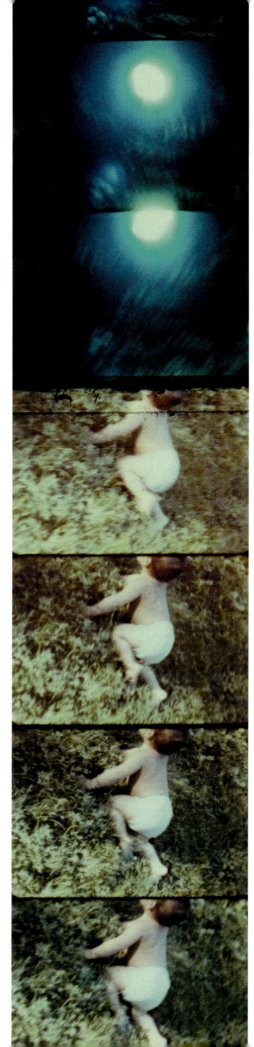

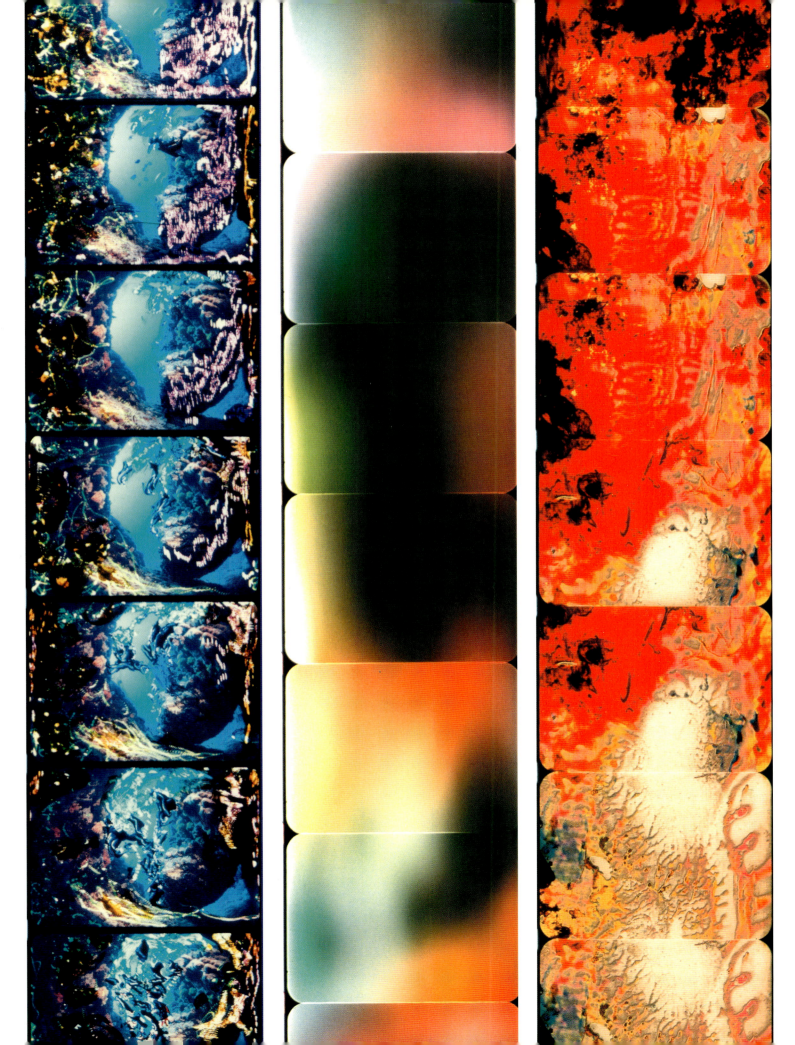

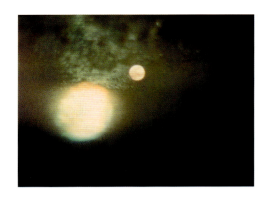

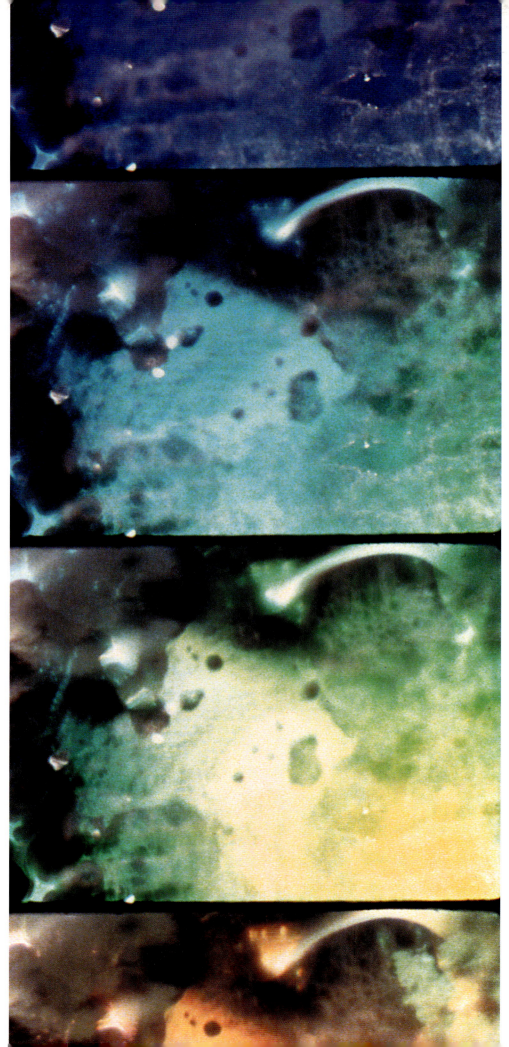

THIS PAGE AND OPPOSITE
Stills from 'Castro Street' (1966)
Fusing impressionistic diary methods and collage
principles, California's Bruce Baillie transformed
roadside images of suburban and rural America
into this landmark experimental work. No
dialogue or voice-over is included, but the film
finds a form of cinematic poetry where rhyming
structures and masculine and feminine
principles become organizing principles.

"Imagine an eye unruled by man-made laws of perspective; an eye unprejudiced by compositional logic; an eye which does not respond to the name of everything, but which must know each new object encountered in life through an adventure of perception."

Stan Brakhage

"Film images are more hallucinatory than still photographs or any others. This kind of drug-related pleasure has to be considered too. I like to have the ecstasy of analysis. An ecstasy of analysis is an odd state and an analysis of ecstasy seems like a waste of a good time."

Michael Snow

script of sorts. "The assignment," Baillie said later, "was not to make a beautiful film, but rather to make a document about this inner passage ... the evolution of consciousness through which every man and woman must go."

By contrast, Sweden's Gunvor Nelson achieves a sublime lyrical quality in her own work, which includes the films *Red Shift* (1984), *Frame Line* (1984), and *Light Years* (1987). Yet she generally eschews the improvisatory style that is so common in the lyrical genre and works instead like a jeweler, carefully carving out incisive, measured rhythms and structures. Thus her films achieve a crystalline beauty that still manages to express, as Steve Anker, dean of the School of Film/Video at CalArts, writes, "an interior world inhabited by haunting memories and richly expressive textures."

Expressing an "interior world," as Anker suggests, through a poetic cinematic language has not only become the hallmark of the lyrical genre, but the central preoccupation of hundreds of filmmakers worldwide. They range from the calculated efforts of Daniel Barnett and Guy Sherwin to the more gestural approach of Antonio DeBernardi and Max Almy; from the playful whimsy of Joyce Wieland and Takahiko Iimura to the intensely introspective efforts of Matthias Müller, Leighton Pierce, and Bill Viola.

For many of these filmmakers and videographers, the image finds a particular state of grace when it moves closer to the rhyming structure of minimalist music, where repetition and silence create a dynamic state of continuance. As a result, these films can often promote a state of transcendence, where literal meanings are destabilized and colors, rhythms, and forms speak directly to the body. "Freely, beautifully, they sing the physical world," writes Jonas Mekas of such films. "Its texture, its colors, its movements; they speak in little bursts of memories, reflections, and meditations."

Phil Solomon, in particular, makes films that do away with cuts—and the frame—altogether. As he says, his hope is that he can make films that "pour out like silver" and achieve a kind of "oceanic consciousness."

ABOVE
Still from 'American Falls' (2008–)
Solomon, a protégé of Brakhage, continues the exploration of the optical printer, where footage is degraded to such a degree that it "stops referring back to the referent," as Solomon says. The result is a shimmering symphony of silver particles that ebb and flow with surprising grace.

TOP
Still from 'The Snowman' (1995)
Phil Solomon used an optical printer to break down found home movies to the point where the film's natural decomposition alternatively suggests snow and rain. The result is a succession of careful rhythms and dissolving figures that becomes a deeply moving meditation on death and decay.

RIGHT
Still from 'Seasons ... ' (2002)
This is the final collaboration (of three films) between Stan Brakhage and Phil Solomon.

And indeed, that is just what they do. Whether he is using found or original footage, he generally uses an optical printer to rework the material until it begins to fragment and achieve a rich tangible texture. Once abstracted, his images tend to resemble waterfalls of swimming crystals, with semirecognizable figures appearing and disappearing into pure shapes and reliefs. More importantly, the Denver-based artist uses precise rhythmic articulations to bring out the personal themes embedded in the material, which gives them a genuine ghostly power. In describing his film, *What's Out Tonight Is Lost* (1983), he says, "the film began in response to an evaporating relationship, but gradually seeped outward to anticipate other imminent disappearing acts: youth, family, friends, time … I wanted the tonal shifts of the film's surface to act as a barometer of the changes in the emotional weather [of my life]. Navigating the bus in the fog, the lighthouse in disrepair."

Nathaniel Dorsky, on the other hand, refuses to abstract his images, and instead bases his impressionism on montage techniques. His films, which include *Pneuma* (1977–1983), *Variations* (1992–1998), and *Threnody* (2004), invite the viewer into a haunted, totally subjective flow of clean figurative images that tend to be less somber than they are pure. These images—a landscape, a figure writing, a shadow—progress moment by moment, pause by pause, without any deliberate narrative thrust. Yet they convey a purely subjective, yet modernist, sensibility where the form conveys its meaning directly, and fully. Indeed, it would be interesting to compare his films with the photography of Helen Levitt, William Eggleston, or Lee Friedlander, for

ABOVE AND TOP
Stills from 'The Man Who Fell to Earth' (1976)
The UK's Nicolas Roeg was always keenly aware of experimental film practices, and often employed similar ideas in his mainstream films. This film in particular uses a brash hallucinatory style to tell the story of an alien visitor coming to terms with widespread alienation and loneliness on planet Earth.

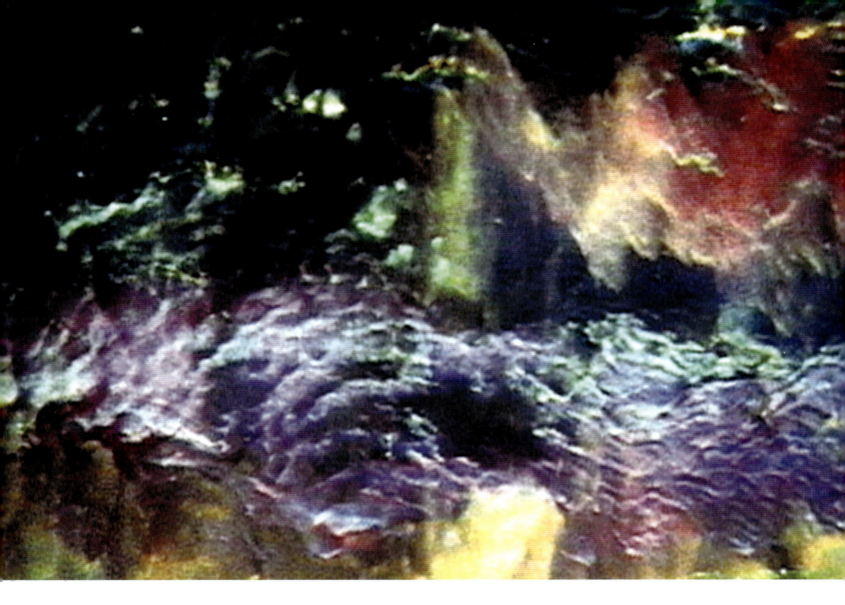

they are self-reflexive yet utterly Zen-like creations. "I want to create films that are
like [sculptural] mobiles," says the filmmaker, "where the images are suspended,
where they have absolutely no relationship to language, and where it becomes more
about *being*."

Epilogue (2005)

Jordan Belson's 50-year career represents one of the most remarkable and
sustained bodies of work in the history of abstract film. His initiation into the genre
came through his exposure to the visual-music experiments of Oskar Fischinger and
his contemporaries, the Whitney brothers. That, in turn, inspired him to seek out
his own cinematic language, which was steeped in both Eastern spirituality and his
own painterly practice. He ultimately designed an optical bench similar to the
Whitneys', where he could produce changing light effects in real time thanks to
small motors and pulleys. The result was a new kind of formless abstraction, which
was largely defined by the viewer's free associations and emotional participation.
"Jordan Belson both preceded and surpassed [Stanley Kubrick's] *2001* in the realm
of cinematic innovations," writes Gene Youngblood. "He is a visionary who has
broken through to the other side; the state of the art need only follow."

Belson's most recent film, *Epilogue* (2005), is a majestic, powerful, sweeping
depiction of morphing colors and moody, misty, prismatic planes, which are

animated to Sergei Rachmaninoff's *Isle of the Dead Opus 29*. Here gaseous clouds build and disappear while nebulous forms create shimmering glissandos of sparks and lavalike pools. As with many of his films, most notably his masterpiece, *Samadhi* (1967), it has a symmetrical structure, with centered compositions, and circular, planetlike shapes reacting to spirals of energy. It feels familiar and utterly real, often suggesting a cosmology, and yet it is also nonobjective to the core.

Nonetheless, *Epilogue* was not designed to function as a meditation tool, as some have assumed. Rather, like most of Belson's films, it was designed to stand on its own, as both a reflection and an expression of Belson's deepest feelings. "[His] is more of a message or philosophical reflection of life, death, and the universe," writes author Ying Tan. "[It is] a trip into outer/inner space."

"[My film] is not to be seen but experienced."
Jordan Belson

The City Symphony, the Essay, and the Landscape Film

While the "city symphony" generally refers to a small number of films that were made in the early part of the 20th Century, these films reflect a much larger trend of urban anthropology that percolates through the entire canon of art filmmaking—from the neorealist's use of locations as metaphors for emotional states to structuralism's radical mapping of urban topographies as a reflection of human thought patterns.

The form technically began with the efforts of documentary filmmakers who were looking to create more poetic, impressionistic portraits of locations without the crutch of didactic voice-overs. Painter Charles Sheeler and photographer Paul Strand helped put the genre in motion in 1921, when they composed *Manhatta*, a short film inspired by a poem by Walt Whitman. Here the filmmakers enter into a kind of communion with the urban environment through a gentle ebb and flow of images, which look and feel like a series of still photographs.

Similarly, Robert J. Flaherty, who had already achieved a significant reputation as a documentary filmmaker, made his own study of abstract patterns found among the skyscrapers of New York, called *Twenty-Four Dollar Island* (c. 1926), and Alberto Cavalcanti made *Rien que les heures* (1926), a seminal documentary that uses the frame of 24 hours to explore Paris and its many facets. The latter, in particular, inspired a host of imitators, most notably Walter Ruttmann's spectacular *Berlin: Die Sinfonie der Großstadt* (*Berlin: Symphony of a Great City*, 1927), a vibrant experimental documentary that shares Cavalcanti's overt socialism, yet offers a more radical visual expression.

Dziga Vertov, on the other hand, believed that the language of the documentary—its believability and access to "truth"—would allow him to advance specific Marxist theories. Thus, with his city symphony, *Chelovek s kino-apparatom* (*Man with a Movie Camera*, 1929), we follow the efforts of a cameraman attempting to capture a day in the life of the Soviet Union, which in turn mirrors the artistic process itself, where "the work" is exalted and celebrated. That, in turn, inspired France's Jean Rouch, who attempted to use an anthropological model in *Chronique d'un été* (*Chronicle of a Summer*, 1961) as "an act of provocation," as he once famously said. (That film, in particular, had a profound effect on Jean-Luc Godard and the French New Wave.)

Since then, the city symphony has taken on many guises, ranging from the jazzlike expressionism of Shirley Clarke, Jules Engel, Marie Menken, and Rudy

ABOVE
Still from 'Skyscraper Symphony' (1929)
Robert Florey was inspired by Walter Ruttmann's portrait of Berlin to make a similar film about New York, where he concentrates on blue-collar workers.

OPPOSITE
Collage from 'Berlin: Symphony of a Great City' (1927)
Germany's Walter Ruttmann was a pioneer in the burgeoning abstract-cinema movement of the 1920s. But with this film he concentrated on the subtle impressions and rhythms found in his native city, without conventional narration or didactic material.

"One could tell a story by images alone, without words, pure as poetry."

Michelangelo Antonioni

THIS PAGE
Stills from 'Manhatta' (1921)
Photographer Paul Strand and painter Charles Sheeler helped set the city-symphony genre in motion with this poetic study of New York City. Each of the film's 65 static shots adds to an overall impression without any obvious narrative structure.

OPPOSITE
**Poster for 'Man with a Movie Camera'
('Chelovek s kino-apparatom', 1929)**

"I think it's impossible to separate a work's social and formal aspects. My films usually begin with the 'discovery' of a real place or location that I find compelling for reasons I'm unable to explain."

Mark Lewis

ABOVE AND OPPOSITE
Stills from 'Man with a Movie Camera'
('Chelovek s kino-apparatom', 1929)
Given its story of a cameraman touring the Soviet
Union in search of imagery, Dziga Vertov's
landmark documentary was initially designed as
a propaganda film. Yet its obvious self-reflexive
nature was also meant to have distinct Marxist
readings. which made it a touchstone for avant-
garde debates.

ABOVE AND LEFT
Stills from 'Metropolis' (1927)
While in New York City, Germany's Fritz Lang conceived of this film as a "battle between modern science and occultism," where the division between workers and owners would be mythologized. Thus, while being an exemplar of German expressionist cinema, it's also a theatrical antecedent to the city-symphony genre.

Stills from 'Skyscraper' (1960)
A former dancer who studied film with Hans Richter, New York's Shirley Clarke turned to socially conscious documentary forms in the 1960s. For this Academy Award–nominated film, she takes a lyrical look at the construction of a building at 666 5th Avenue, with carefully modulated tones of light and shadow.

Stills from 'Skyscraper' (1960)

BOTTOM LEFT

Still from 'Shift' (1972–74)

For this film Gehr began with a view from high above a busy street, which he shot with extreme angles and variable speeds. While seemingly random, the effects nonetheless appear to be synchronized to the music of honking horns, breaks, and gears, which in turn underscores the presence of the camera.

BOTTOM RIGHT

Still from 'Serene Velocity' (1970)

Gehr's most famous film consists of static shots taken inside an institutional hallway at night. Thus over the course of the film, the scene shifts aggressively between focal lengths to both flatten the image and call attention to representation.

BELOW

Still from 'Reverberation' (1969, revised 1986)

As a key figure in the structuralist movement of the 1970s, New York–based Ernie Gehr often used the city as his primary subject, which in turn allowed him to explore the nature of seeing.

Burkhardt to the sprawling 70mm epics of Godfrey Reggio, Ron Fricke, and Velu Viswanadhan; from recent omnibus films such as *Visions of Europe* (2004), by 25 international directors, to the quiet, contemplative films of personal filmmakers such as Jim Jennings, Walid Ra'ad, and Jaan Toomik.

Indeed, the city symphony has become so popular within avant-garde circles that it has come to "underwrite the entire experimental film exercise," as Paul Arthur writes. This is not only because of what the city represents, but also because it provides a fitting backdrop for experiments in empiricism and epistemology.

That was particularly true for the structuralist filmmakers of the 1960s and 1970s. Like Vertov, these filmmakers recorded views of the city in such a way that the recording process itself took on new meanings. Ernie Gehr made a number of fascinating films that intensified city views to the point where the viewer could almost "see and hear the whirling of atoms beneath the image," as Michael Snow once described his *Reverberation* (1969). Indeed, that was his goal: to make those "whirling atoms" the very subject of his films. And he did that by reducing his films down to specific camera functions. He manipulated the focal lengths on a zoom lens for *Serene Velocity* (1970), which creates an astonishingly impressionistic view of a hallway, and *Wait* (1968) may be the first movie to be composed entirely out of manipulating f-stops.

Aside from being a modernist exercise in letting the medium speak its own language, Gehr's films also can be seen as both personal expressions and allegories for human perception. His *Still* (1969–1971) depicts a continuous, restless stare out of an apartment window that shifts the focus away from a seemingly random view of passing cars and pedestrians to an intense meditation on Gehr's presence behind the camera. As Richard Foreman describes the film, "Gehr has succeeded in making the first objectification-of-atmosphere film in which objects and relationships between them end up *radiating* the mood."

Hollis Frampton, Peter Hutton, Daniel Eisenberg, Larry Gottheim, David Hall, Lisl Ponger, and Rüdiger Neumann have since brought a similar reductive/

conceptual approach to their films, where mapping and mathematical equations are used to highlight the observational and taxonomical quality of the film recording. Hans Scheugl, for instance, used exactly 30 meters of film to cover a street in Vienna with the same dimensions.

Others employ a more poetic approach, one that remains formally complex but uses montage techniques to evoke a mood or feeling. Scotland's Margaret Tait invoked Federico García Lorca's idea of "stalking the image" in describing her own poetic city symphonies, including *Rose Street* (1956). For her, the choice of precise imagery has a direct corollary in the poet's endless search for the exact word or phrase. "In poetry," she said, "something else happens. Hard to say what it is. Let's say soul or spirit, an empathy with whatever it is that's dwelt upon."

Similarly, Robert Beavers, who was mentored by Gregory J. Markopoulos, fills his delicate, contemplative films with metonymies—a landscape, a suitcase, a human figure, a color—to achieve a dense emotional complex. *Efpsychi* (1983–1996) draws a direct parallel between classical figuration—the male visage—and various streets in Athens, which are named after famous playwrights. As a result, he creates deeply contemplative moods that seem to transform figure and place into a transcendent time/space continuum. "The search is for a reality with the individual physiognomy," explained Beavers, "for a generous physicality that will not fade."

Still from 'This Side of Paradise' (1991)
While in Germany shortly before the wall came down, Gehr took his camera to common flea markets, where he focused primarily on the reflections in street puddles as a way to explore figure/ground contrast.

"Traditional and established avant-garde film teaches film to be an image, a representation. But film is a real thing and as a real thing it is not imitation. It does not reflect on life, it embodies the life of the mind."
Ernie Gehr

ABOVE
Still from 'Efpsychi' (1983–1996)
As mentored by Gregory Markopoulos, Robert Beavers brings a similar jewel-like precision to his meditative films. Here he combines images of a young man, mostly shot in close-up, with old buildings in the market quarter of Athens, where each street is named after a Greek playwright. Thus history seems to impose itself on the figure, which undergoes intensive scrutiny.

LEFT
Still from 'Diminished Frame' (1970–2001)
Filmed in West Berlin, this film by Robert Beavers attempts to explore a sense of the past by using black-and-white footage of cityscapes, and combining them with a progression of color filters placed in the camera's aperture. "It's the space of the city," said Beavers, "and of the filmmaker."

RIGHT
Still from 'Regen' (1929)
Made by Dutchman Joris Ivens, one of cinema's most celebrated documentarians, this film uses a narrative structure of tempo, rhythm, and intensity, where light rainfall eventually leads to a torrent of water.

BOTTOM
Still from 'Vacancy' (1998)
Using found and original footage, Matthias Müller, one of Germany's most accomplished collage/essay artists, creates a moving portrait of Brasilia, the city of hope, which becomes a mirror for the narrator's own confrontation with death.

ABOVE AND OPPOSITE TOP
Stills from 'La Jetée' (1962)
Chris Marker's meditation on the tension between past, present, and future was one of the landmark underground films of the 1960s and later inspired Terry Gilliam's *Twelve Monkeys* (1995). It was made entirely out of still photographs and tells the story of a future generation of scientists who seek to understand the world's destruction by sending a man first into the past and then into the future.

Germany's Matthias Müller, on the other hand, makes his own deeply personal films that often use specific locations as inspiration for larger emotional and philosophical inquiries. His *Pensão Globo* (1997) follows a shadowy protagonist through Lisbon, the city of Fado (fate), to find a visual corollary to the fragmented memories of a man dying of AIDS. Conversely, *Vacancy* (1998) draws a parallel between Brasilia, the failed utopia, and the ruminations of a thoughtful narrator who fills the audio track with quotes by Samuel Beckett, Italo Calvino, and others. In the process, the film becomes a story about a man trying—and failing—to find himself.

Films such as these also fall under the heading of "the essay film," which blends the expressiveness of the lyrical film with the personal aspects of the autobiographical genre. Generally speaking, the essay film consists of a director and cameraman relating his or her experiences via voice-over narration while presenting an impressionistic view of a physical or metaphoric journey. But essay films can also verge on the abstract, as in the affecting films of Daniel Eisenberg, Peter Hutton, and Irit Batsry, where unstaged scenes are composed without commentary or voice-overs.

In terms of the former, France's Chris Marker deserves special attention. Born in 1921, he was an accomplished author and essay-style filmmaker long before he made *La Jetée* (1962), the 28-minute film that brought him international attention.

(That film uses still photographs—with matching eye lines, master shots, close-ups, dissolves, and fades—to create a fictional sci-fi fable about memory and love.) His travelogues of the late 1950s, *Dimanche à Pekin* (1956) and *Lettre de Sibérie* (1957), are defined by the filmmaker's subjectivity, where he explores foreign lands while making astute observations along the way. Yet it is not his adventures that move the story along, but his ideas, which flutter about, lyrically, spectrally, obsessively, never suggesting answers but always asking questions. As author Catherine Lupton writes in her insightful study of the filmmaker, "Marker's methodology finds echoes in ancient Greek ideals, most notably the concept of selfhood as a constant interior dialogue with the Other; the Socratic principles of rigorous intellectual enquiry by questioning and debate; the centrality of myth and the meaning of artistic creation. [These] are the foundations of Marker's own approach to cinema and other audio-visual media."

His masterwork is *Sans Soleil* (1983), a film that ostensibly follows a cynical, disillusioned filmmaker as he becomes obsessed with filming what he calls the "two extremes of survival," namely Japan and Africa. Yet throughout his journey, he continually questions the very meaning of images, both those playing on the screen and those lodged in our collective memories—from Alfred Hitchcock's *Vertigo* (1958) to revolutionary struggles worldwide. In that sense the film is marked by dialectical

ABOVE
Still from 'London' (1994)
One of the UK's best-known landscape/essay artists, Patrick Keiller routinely explores the historical and metaphorical interpretations of specific locations with a sly wit and an eye for socioeconomic signifiers. Here he digs into the troubled background of his native city in a way that recalls the Greek definition of *nostalgia*, meaning: "the wounds of returning."

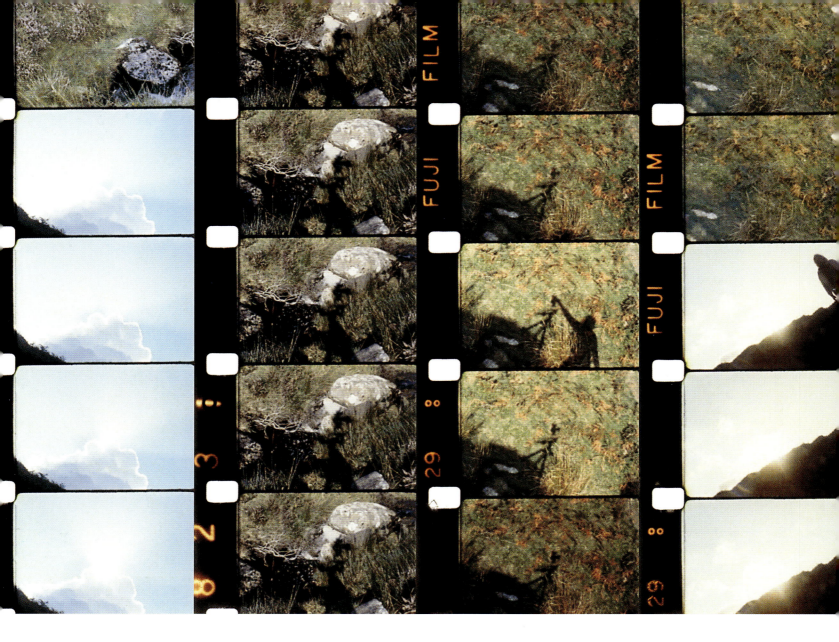

ABOVE
Film Strips from 'Seven Days' (1974)
Arguably the UK's most important landscape filmmaker, Chris Welsby used time-lapse photography and an equatorial stand so that his camera always pointed at its own shadow over the course of a week. As a result, the film is shaped not by the filmmaker's intent, but by the way the technology reacts to nature.

BELOW
Still from 'Shoreline' (1977)
Using six 16mm projectors to depict a single panorama, Welsby draws attention to the noise and mechanical nature of the projectors themselves, which, ironically, drown out the serene nature of the image depicted.

OPPOSITE
Stills from 'One Way Boogie Woogie/27 Years Later' (1977/2004)
For this project California's James Benning returned to Milwaukee, where he shot a 60-minute film looking at the city's industrial landscape with individual 1-minute shots, and recreated the exact same film 27 years later, connecting the two films back-to-back.

extremes in both sound and picture, from male and female narrators to past and present temporal modes and theoretical propositions and contradictions. "Each step of this imaginary dialogue aims to create a third voice out of the meeting of the first two, which is distinct from them," Marker said. "I don't claim to have succeeded in making a dialectical film, but for once I've tried to give the spectator, by means of the montage, their own commentary."

A handful of filmmakers have brought their own, unique stamp to the essay film, although with mixed results. Daniel Eisenberg, Patrick Keiller, and Werner Herzog have imbued it with a heady intellectual rigor, while Robert Frank, John Jost, Mark Rappaport, and Paul Cox have preferred to use a looser, lyrical approach, where sense impressions and fragments are woven together into an expressive whole.

At this point the city symphony and the essay genres come together in a related form known as the landscape film. Like its painterly counterpart, the landscape tradition explores both subjective and objective renderings of specific natural locations. Renaissance painters were known to portray the land as emotional states, as in J.M.W. Turner's storm clouds or seascapes. (That also holds true for the hundreds of narrative filmmakers who use backdrops to mirror a character's state of being.) But with the conceptual strategies of 1970s experimental film, landscape filmmakers took that idea a step further by drawing a direct corollary between the recording of a landscape and cognition, where the process of gathering empirical data is inseparable from the meaning of that data. Dozens of filmmakers have attempted to realize that idea in their own experimental filmmaking practices, including Michael Snow in Canada, Gary Beydler and Bill Viola in the United States, Artavazd Peleshyan in Armenia, and a wide range of British artists including Chris Welsby, William Raban, David Crosswaite, and Annabel Nicholson.

Welsby, in particular, has tried to make films that are outside his own influence altogether, where the film is quite literally the result of natural forces. His classic, *Seven Days* (1974), is defined entirely by how the camera, which was set on an equatorial mount, reacts to both weather changes and the Earth's movement. And, more recently, he has moved into the realm of interactive installation, where he uses advanced technologies not only to record and display landscapes in real time, but to create beguiling visualizations that remain in a continual state of flux. *Trees in Winter* (2006) feeds the input of current weather conditions into a software program, which in turn dictates the editing of three alternating views of a treescape in real time. Thus the representation of nature is manipulated by nature itself, and no single image ever repeats.

By contrast, America's James Benning prefers a durational approach, where specific locations are presented with a static camera, without any commentary or editorializing whatsoever. His films *El Valley Centro* (2000), *Sogobi* (2001), and *Los* (2001) present a series of 35 perfectly composed landscapes found in urban and rural areas of Southern California. Each of these landscapes remains on screen for exactly 2 ½ minutes. Thus, Benning's tableaux can be seen as a flip side to the use of mise-en-scène in expressionist cinema, where locations are used to telegraph specific feelings and ideas defined by the filmmaker. "We are so used to seeing iconic landscapes in nature films," argues Benning, "that we've stopped looking at all the detail in the background."

That idea finds its fullest realization in recent installation work, where the viewer quite literally steps into the illusion of another place and time. Craigie Horsfield's installation piece, *El Hierro Conversation* (2002), features four omnidirectional views

Still from 'All of My Life' (1966)
A minor masterpiece, Bruce Baillie's film shows little more than a single tracking shot along a flower-covered fence to the tune of Ella Fitzgerald's song of the same name. While minimalist in approach, the staccato rhythms of the fence's wooden slats mimic the song's beat, while Fitzgerald's vocals touch on themes of waiting.

"In my films I'm very aware of recording a place over time and how that makes you understand a place. Once you've been watching something for a while you become aware of it differently. I could show you a photograph of a place but it's not the same as seeing it over time."

James Benning

from an intersection in a small village in the Canary Islands. These four views are projected simultaneously onto four walls in a gallery for an entire day (nine hours and 17 minutes).

Pat O'Neill, Bruce Baillie, Ken Kobland, Steve Beck, and Jeremy Blake tend to abstract their images through optical printers and synthesizers in an attempt to create a subjective view of a particular location. Thus urban and rural landscapes are transformed into discrete, plastic objects. Michel Gondry's clever, and surprisingly subtle, *Star Guitar* (2002) transforms an utterly passive, even meditative view of a pastoral landscape as seen from a moving train into a visual ballet via digital manipulation. Here bridges, telephone lines, and the rush of trees begin to percolate and dance in time with the soundtrack. And yet the entire image remains utterly faithful and representational.

This recent work has been created in the shadow of the Internet, which has triggered new concerns with physical and intellectual space. Today film and video makers are starting to rethink the city symphony through the lens of surveillance, social determinants, and notions of the Panopticon. Wolfgang Staehle's now-legendary surveillance of New York's World Trade Center shortly before and during the attacks of 9/11 stand as a landmark here. But other contemporary artists are continuing to bring their own, unique approaches to the city symphony. These

Still from '2001' (2001)
Germany's Wolfgang Staehle took on Warhol's durational epic, *Empire* (1964), by creating a live feed from across New York's harbor for an entire month. Thus he coincidentally captured the attacks on the World Trade Center on 9/11, which were fed to monitors in a gallery and on the Web.

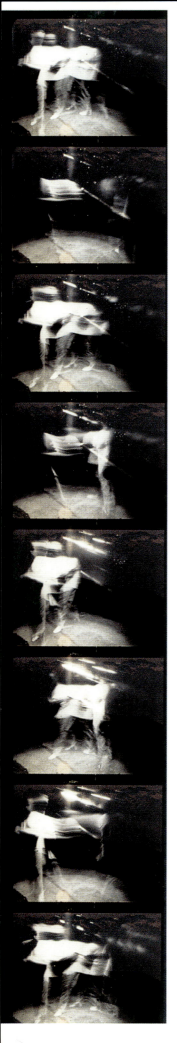
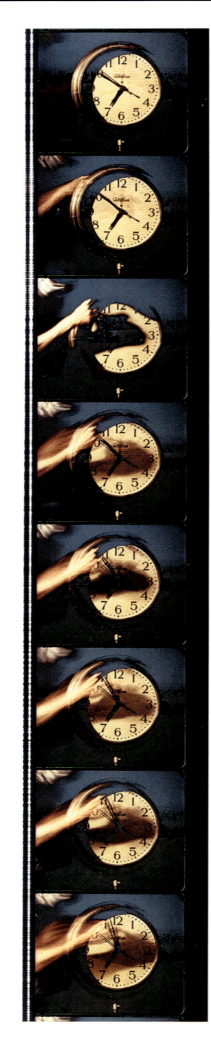
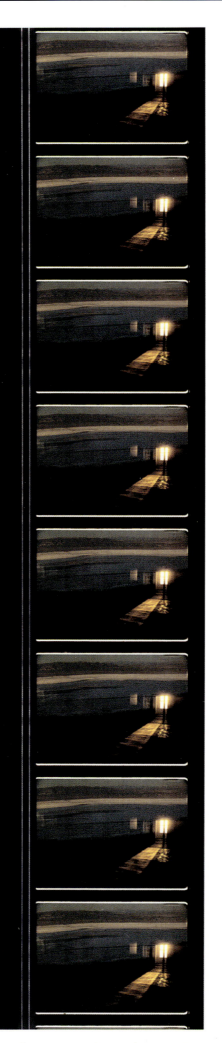
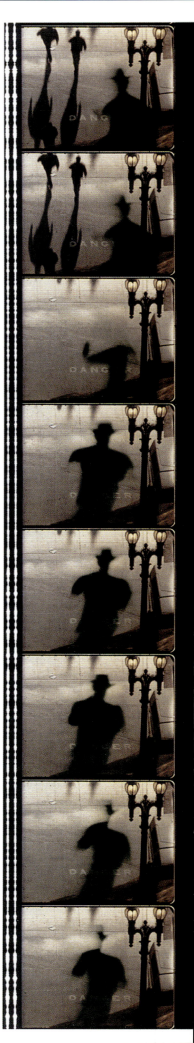

include Jane and Louise Wilson and Hamish Fulton in the United Kingdom, Sarah Morris and Stephen Dean in the United States, Melik Ohanian in France, Francis Alÿs in Mexico, Masaki Fujihata in Japan, Joachim Koester in Denmark and Gustav Deutsch and Thomas Korschil in Austria.

The Decay of Fiction (2002)

As the director of the special-effects house Lookout Mountain Films in Los Angeles, which counts George Lucas as a client, Pat O'Neill has developed formidable skills as an optical technician. His short and full-length experimental films tend to be more visually complex than the work of many of his peers, with exceedingly lush visuals and tightly composed—and composited—frames. "He has approached filmmaking as a bricoleur," writes John G. Hanhardt, "shaping seamless moving images that echo the narratives, myths, and stories embedded in the everyday culture of Los Angeles and its suburban surroundings."

Indeed, O'Neill's 40-year career as an experimental filmmaker falls somewhere between fine-art collage and landscape filmmaking. His major statement in that area is *Water and Power* (1989), a full-length film that was the result of a new motion-control system designed by Mark Mandel. That allowed him to animate and repeat camera movements on all four axes so that he could fuse different temporal periods—both past and present—into simultaneous overlaps. Specifically, he pulled scenes from classic Hollywood films, such as Edgar G. Ulmer's *Detour* (1945), and overlaid them with his own original material shot at the same location. "Every moment [in real life] is full of memories of the present and the expectation of the future," said O'Neill. "There is always your mind's eye and what you are actually seeing."

That idea finds its fullest realization in *The Decay of Fiction* (2002), a film that treats the site of Los Angeles's Ambassador Hotel as a giant camera obscura, continually projecting its imagined past onto its present interior. For that film, O'Neill shot several hours of footage inside the hotel and then used a computer to accurately record the precise position and movements of his camera setups and transpose them onto camera movements shot inside a studio. Thus he was able to "ghost in" fictional scenes with actors performing a 1940s-style film noir, complete with mob payoffs, ill-fated love affairs, and murder. The result is a haunting meditation on both time and space that suggests a host of art-historical references, including the statuary of George Segal and the entire canon of film noir. "I would say that I work abstractly," said O'Neill, "in that meaning for me has more to do with the relationship between parts than the individual parts themselves. But I retain an oblique connection to narrative and storytelling."

"The process of representing the landscape, in either a single screen work or an installation, is not to be seen as separate from nature, but viewed instead as part of a more symbiotic model in which technology and nature are both viewed as interrelated parts of a larger gestalt."

Chris Welsby

ABOVE AND TOP
Stills from 'Colours of this Time' (1972)
The UK's William Raban was another essential figure in the structuralist movement of the period. Here the camera shutter was open for the entire 16-hour period of filming, so a complete record of the changing landscape was made rather than a partial one.

OPPOSITE
Film Strips from 'Water and Power' (1989)
Using a new motion-control system that allowed him to animate and repeat camera movements on all four axes, Pat O'Neill pulled scenes from classic Hollywood films and overlaid them with new footage shot at the same location. In this way he could fuse different temporal periods—both past and present—into simultaneous overlaps.

Temps Mort, Tableau, and Duration

In 1943 Maya Deren and her collaborator, Alexander Hammid, created one of the true masterpieces of art cinema, *Meshes of the Afternoon*, an early experiment in subjective temporal modes. Unfortunately for Deren and Hammid, that film was often mischaracterized as a surrealist effort because it depicts a heady dream state, where a woman (Deren) enters into, and relives, three identical moments filled with potent symbols—most notably knives, keys, and mirrors. Yet Deren rejected the surrealist label, saying that surrealism "denies the rigors and disciplines of the art instrument," and it fails to recognize that great works of art and science are the result of intense, purposeful studies. "If all men had agreed with the realists and the romantics," she added, "to describe, exalt, and extend the natural condition, there would be no such thing as science, philosophy, or art."

Her interest in laying bare the inherent structures of the medium led her to the conclusion that just because a screen is a two-dimensional surface, it doesn't have to be seen as a (frozen) painterly canvas defined by composition and figuration. "Because," as she pointed out, "it is not the way anything is at a given moment that is important in film, it's what it's doing, how it's *becoming*. In other words, [film is a] composition *over time*, rather than within a space, which is important. In this sense I say, structurally, it is much more comparable to time forms, including poetry."

That led her to the notion that every film proceeds via two simultaneous progressions: a horizontal one and a vertical one. The former deals with character and cause-and-effect, while the latter deals with mood, tone, and rhythm. (In many ways, that was very much in keeping with the Greek notion of *kairos* and *chronos*, or emotional time versus measured time.) Thus Deren began to punctuate her narratives with *temps mort* (dead time) in an attempt to shift the progression from horizontal to vertical.

Bertolt Brecht used a similar idea in his theatrical productions as a form of distancing, where a pause pushes the viewer outside the fiction and allows for moments of reflection. Yet whereas Brecht (and by extension Godard) overfilled his tangents with an abundance of signifiers, *temps mort* attempts to underfill them with ambiguity and absence. Here, as the camera turns away and focuses on extradiegetic landscapes and empty rooms, it focuses on atmosphere, which opens up and allows for the projection of the viewer's own thoughts and feelings.

ABOVE
Painting by Peter Greenaway for 'The Falls' (1980)

OPPOSITE
Portrait of Maya Deren (circa 1950)

"The distinction of art is that it is neither simply an expression, of pain for example, nor an impression of pain. But it is a form that creates pain—or whatever emotional intent."

Maya Deren

Carl Theodor Dreyer, Victor Sjöström, and Kenji Mizoguchi used sustained shots to great effect in the 1930s, but the technique really came into fashion with both the neorealist movement of the 1940s and 1950s and the "direct" cinema of Robert Frank, John Cassavetes, and Shirley Clark. *Viaggio in Italia* (*Journey to Italy*, 1954) by Roberto Rossellini successfully conveys the emotional bankruptcy of its characters almost entirely through images of empty rooms, barren landscapes, and negative space. As David Bordwell writes, "between neorealism, with its gap-filled narratives and unexpected longueurs, and the blank surfaces and diminuendo pacing of Antonioni's *L'avventura* (1960), filmic storytelling changed significantly. Dramas began excising melodrama, moving closer to the spacious rhythms of the modern novel."

Indeed, Italy's Michelangelo Antonioni found his style through his initial work as a neorealist, but that led him to a more reflective, interior style of filmmaking that was closer to the stream of consciousness of literary models. As he said, "The only useful way to adhere to [the rules of] neorealism is to take an interest in the interior rather than in the exterior—to express sentiments before choosing decors. [In other words] some filmmakers decide to tell a story and then choose a decor that suits it best. With me it works the other way around: there's some landscape, some place where I want to shoot, and out of that develops the theme of my films."

Most of his films deal with characters suffering from intense emotional states, yet they rarely, if ever, express themselves—which is the ideal condition for an effective *temps mort*. Here the filmmaker uses a wholly intuitive camera to continually scan his subjects, as if the camera itself wants to possess something that it cannot, while arresting the narrative repeatedly to introduce moments of vertical progression. "We know that underneath the displayed image," said the director in 1964, "there is another—one more faithful to reality. And underneath this second there is a third one, and a fourth under the previous one. All the way to the true image of that reality, absolute, mysterious, that nobody will see. Or all the way to the dissolution of reality. Abstract cinema, therefore, would make sense."

ABOVE AND TOP
Stills from 'La Passion de Jeanne d'Arc' (1928)
Using concise composition, *temps mort*, and tableaux to emphasize a painterly quality, Carl Theodor Dreyer's version of the Joan of Arc story remains one of the most effective renditions of the tale.

RIGHT
Still from 'Meshes of the Afternoon' (1943)
Maya Deren and Alexander Hammid's film uses in-camera effects and concise editing to split the protagonist, played by Deren, into four versions of herself, each with her own desires, fantasies, and memories. The result is a complex study of the human psyche, which has since been recognized as one of the essential landmarks of experimental-film history.

'Complex study of the human psyche!...'

Antonioni's use of *temps mort* was indeed an attempt at a more abstract narrative cinema, and his films often approached the sheer lyrical quality of visual music. By contrast, Belgium's Chantal Akerman used *temps mort* to challenge the patriarchal tendencies of mainstream cinema and its conventions. Her highly influential film *Jeanne Dielman, 23 Quai du Commerce, 1080 Bruxelles* (1975) uses the sustained shot to show us the *actual* day-to-day existence of a working-class woman who has to resort to prostitution to pay the rent. Here Akerman deliberately expands all those moments that would normally be cut from a Hollywood film—the mundane and the common—and does the reverse with the most dramatic elements, including sex scenes and the eventual murder of a john, which are left off screen. That gives the viewer a stronger sense of the emptiness of Dielman's life, rather than the manipulative approach of most Hollywood productions.

Temps mort* has also been explored with great success by the French filmmakers Robert Bresson, Alain Resnais, and Jean-Marie Straub and Danièle Huillet in the 1950s and 1960s, and they in turn inspired at least three generations of Europeans, including Miklós Jancsó, Wim Wenders, Aki Kaurismäki, Theo Angelopoulos, and Abbas Kiarostami. But it was, and still is, in more oppressive territories, such as the Middle East and Asia, where *temps mort* has flourished in recent years. For filmmakers such as Satyajit Ray, Makoto Shinozaki, Shinji Aoyama, and a host of

Still from 'L'avventura' (1960)
The first part of Michelangelo Antonioni's urban trilogy finds two friends, played by Monica Vitti and Gabriele Ferzetti, who struggle with their feelings after Ferzetti's girlfriend disappears and never returns. Thus the theme of absence becomes an organizing principle for the film, which the director exploits through visual tangents and narrative lapses.

"I always mistrust everything that I see, everything that an image shows me. Because I imagine what's beyond it, and what's beyond an image can't be known."
Michelangelo Antonioni

① HOLD FIELD Ⓐ FOR 30 SECS.
② HOLD FIELD Ⓑ FOR 30 SECS
③ HOLD FIELD Ⓒ (or as close-in as you can make it) FOR 30 SECS.

ABOVE, LEFT AND RIGHT
Preproduction Sketches for 'Vertical Features Remake' (1978)
A humorous take on postmodern cinema, Peter Greenaway's film contains four films-within-a-film. But the overall idea is to create a film that is a reconstruction of deliberate directions that never reach a conclusion due to conflicting interpretations of the same instructions.

OPPOSITE BOTTOM
Still from 'The Draughtsman's Contract' (1982)
A self-reflexive period piece where a wealthy daughter hires a painter to create drawings from tableaux vivants, which leads to sexual exploits and a complex conflict between representation and reality.

"Hide the ideas, but so that people find them. The most important will be the most hidden."

Robert Bresson

contemporary filmmakers such as Wong Kar-wai, Hou Hsiao-Hsien, Cui Zi En, and Jia Zhangke, the technique of withholding information allows them not only to tell poignant stories of the poor and the exploited, but also to avoid government censorship. As critic Donald Richie writes, the Japanese in particular find a direct corollary between the tableau and the Japanese tradition of formal presentation, which, he says, "gives form—and life—to *everything*, including nature itself."

One of the qualities of the tableau is that, amid all its strict formalism and ordered presentation, it can also be a subversive strategy. Russia's Sergei Parajanov, in particular, considered the single view of the camera to be the sole province of the bourgeoisie (much like the impressionists before him). Therefore, a more frontal, hierarchical, tableau-style image was preferable because it would offer a more iconic image that would be closer to folk art, or the art of the people. In his films the image seems to be decorated from top to bottom, as opposed to foreground to background, and thus, like folk art, it not only moves away from a singular viewpoint as in perspective drawing, but retains a certain amount of whimsy. As Jonathan Rosenbaum describes Parajanov's masterpiece, *Sayat Nova* (*The Color of Pomegranates*, 1968), "the images giggle with delight."

That idea took a postmodern turn within the artistic milieu of the 1970s and 1980s, when "quoting" paintings became a kind of end in itself. That is when dozens of art-house filmmakers such as Jean-Luc Godard, Eric Rohmer, Derek Jarman, Raúl Ruiz, and Peter Greenaway used the technique to punctuate their narratives with self-reflexive, painterly references that were designed to throw the entire film into a series of visual puns. Ruiz used the tableau to great effect in his *L'Hypothèse du tableau volé* (*The Hypothesis of the Stolen Painting*, 1979), a film that follows a character as he recreates a number of paintings as tableaux vivants to solve a crime. By doing so, he attempts to use the process of reproducing a reproduction of reality as "an illustration," as he says, "or even proof, of the eternal return."

A similar approach can also be found in the realm of experimental film, even among filmmakers working with such wildly diverse styles as Jack Smith, James Broughton, Peter Wollen and Laura Mulvey, and Red Grooms and Robert Nelson.

The film *Ein Bild* (*An Image*, 1983) by Germany's Harun Farocki is composed of a series of tracking shots where the camera repeatedly moves past a "pinup" tableau featuring a beautiful nude perfectly posed in a bedroom setting. Yet in each case, the film crew seems more interested in the technical aspects of the image than in the nude model herself. Thus the production of the image, in the material sense, both mirrors and critiques its own values.

Arguably the most interesting use of the tableau, however, occurred within experimental-film circles in the 1960s and 1970s, when filmmakers not only made entire films of single, sustained shots, but also attempted to destroy the picture plane in the same way that the cubist painters of the early 1900s attempted to overturn easel painting. Hollis Frampton's *Lemon* (1969), Malcolm Le Grice's *Academic Still Life* (1976), Ernie Gehr's *Table* (1976), and Gary Hill's more recent *Still Life* (1999) are intensive studies of individual views that break up and fold back on themselves with surprising elasticity.

That idea leads us to the purest form of filmic tableau, where a single image is presented over the course of an entire film. These works, which flourished in the 1960s and 1970s with both structuralist and Fluxus filmmakers, can be seen as a

ABOVE
Production still from 'The Draughtsman's Contract' (1982)
Director Peter Greenaway, captured in the grid.

ABOVE
Still from 'Jeanne Dielman, 23 Quai du Commerce, 1080 Bruxelles' (1975)
While ostensibly about a widow who supports herself as a prostitute while caring for her son following a court order, Chantal Akerman's film is now seen as a minor masterpiece of 1970s cinema. Rather than exploiting dramatic moments, which are either omitted or played offscreen, Akerman focuses entirely on that which Hollywood films would typically gloss over: the banality of washing the dishes or making a pot of coffee. Thus the woman's plight is made all the more tangible.

RIGHT
Production still for 'Blue' (1993)
Derek Jarman's 50th and final film was a reaction to the news that he was HIV positive. It features no image whatsoever other than a saturated blue color field and a faint silhouette of Jarman, which is combined with a sampling of voice-overs by his friends and loved ones.

direct counterargument to Walter Benjamin's famous statement about the innate difference between painting and film. As he said in 1936, "the painting invites the spectator to contemplation. Before it the spectator can abandon himself to his associations. Before the movie frame, he cannot do so. No sooner has his eye grasped a scene than it is already changed. It cannot be arrested."

Artists of the 1960s, by contrast, believed that they could create a time-based work that would in fact allow the viewer to "abandon himself to his associations." Jack Smith created theater works based on great historical themes, which he performed as static tableaux over the course of an entire night. Similarly, the Fluxus artist Jackson Mac Low proposed a film in 1961 called *Tree* Movie*, which was designed to show a single tree over the course of an entire day. And then came Andy Warhol in 1963 with his own single-subject films, which played for extreme lengths of time. His five-hour *Sleep* (1963), eight-hour *Empire* (1964), and 24-hour *Couch* (1964) were not single, static shots, as many critics have claimed, but edited and looped to give the impression of real time. Thus they were designed to allow the viewer to come and go at random, catching snippets of movement here and there without ever grasping the film's entirety.

Dozens of filmmakers and contemporary artists have since adopted a similar practice, among them Robert Wilson, Daniel Eisenberg, Vincent Grenier, Kutluğ Ataman, Douglas Gordon, Darren Almond, and Ann-Sofi Sidén. There are others who attempt to achieve a similar effect through looping, where individual cinematic moments, however insignificant, are cut into loops and repeated endlessly. Jack Goldstein's *Metro-Goldwyn-Mayer* (1974) was little more than a continuous loop of MGM's famous lion roaring over and over. And his *Shane* (1974) depicted that movie's famous German shepherd barking repeatedly. For Goldstein, a Canadian painter and photographer who exhibited widely throughout the 1970s and 1980s, such tiny moments, snapped up and replayed over and over, deftly highlight certain feelings that are associated with the cinematic experience. *Metro-Goldwyn-Mayer* extends the feeling of anticipation that occurs just before a Hollywood spectacular,

Still from 'Steve Buscemi' (2006)
By shooting 2- to 15-minute static moments, which are looped to play continuously, New York's Robert Wilson creates high-definition video portraits that exist in time and space much like a painting or fine-art photograph. With music by Michael Galasso.

Still from 'The Greeting' (1995)
For this vertically framed video, Bill Viola recreated Pontormo's *Visitation* (1528–1529) by slowing down the action of three women meeting in a public square to near stasis. Thus the scene takes on a painterly temporality.

ABOVE AND TOP
Stills from 'Ein Bild' (1983)
For this exquisite film, the Czech-born, Berlin-based Harun Farocki uses a continual tracking shot to document the production of a German *Playboy* shoot featuring a nude model and a crew of stagehands. Thus the creation of an image, ideal and model, becomes a Marxist deconstruction of the commercialization of desire.

déconstruction of
hollywood ideology!

"Through cinema, time is an island."
Jerome Hill

while *Shane*'s faithful dog symbolizes the distillation of joyous catharsis that is so essential to the Hollywood model.

All of this happened as the hegemony of modernism—its self-reflexiveness, its formalism, its abstraction—was starting to wane. In its place came a new aesthetic born of both minimalism and conceptualism, where the artwork would exist somewhere in between language and image, substance and emptiness. Ed Ruscha's famous deadpan photographic books featuring the most mundane and banal subjects imaginable—parking lots, individual palm trees, backyard swimming pools—serve as a touchstone to the zeitgeist of the period. His images, rendered without commentary, become humorous-yet-impenetrable Zen koans continually oscillating between the absurd and the prosaic.

That coincided with the prevalence of portable video cameras, which not only inspired artists such as Bruce Nauman, Dennis Oppenheim, Chris Burden, Vito Acconci, and Peter Campus to create the absolute antithesis of television proper, but also allowed them to create singular video images that would exist in and of themselves. The American artist John Baldessari videotaped himself making small repetitive hand movements while repeating the phrase "I am making art" in 1971. While deliberately silly, the static quality of the piece offered a sly riposte to both the art world's obsession with gesture and minimalism's insistence on the immediacy of the experience.

Since then the tableau has continued to evolve with both the advancement of digital technologies and a marked return to the narrative potential of the static shot. Both Bruno Munari (*The Card Players*, 1963) and the video artist Bill Viola (*The Greeting*, 1995) anticipated much of today's work in this area by faithfully reproducing classic Renaissance paintings in film and video, respectively, and presenting them as static works. And since then Eve Sussman, Robert Wilson, Jeroen de Rijke and Willem de Rooij, Brian Eno, Marco Brambilla, Daria Martin, Burt Barr, Paul Chan, and Paulette Phillips have created their own "cinematic paintings," as Wilson calls his own work, which operate very much like fine-art, photographic prints.

In Wilson's case, famous actors including Brad Pitt, Isabelle Huppert, and Johnny Depp are "frozen" through high-speed photography, and transformed into living incarnations of famous Renaissance paintings. Mikhail Baryshnikov is depicted as the martyred St. Sebastian, and Winona Ryder resembles the protagonist of Beckett's *Happy Days* (1961). Conversely, the American-Swiss team of Teresa Hubbard and Alexander Birchler create their own, quietly affecting tableau films that marry the aesthetic quality of narrative photography with the affecting subjectivity of *temps mort*. Their *House with Pool* (2004) is a carefully choreographed scenario that portrays the internal lives of two women quietly exploring the aftermath of a house party. Here the shadow of Antonioni looms large as the formal aspects of the film—its modulated atmosphere and camera moves—are used to paint an evocative, psychological space. As Shamim M. Momin writes, "Hubbard and Birchler depict a melancholic, emotionally charged experience that suggests an existential conflict roiling just beneath the calm surface of the familiar."

Stills from 'Zocalo' (1999)
Working with artist Rafael Ortega, the Belgium-born Francis Alÿs focused his camera on Mexico City's most famous public square with a single, unblinking, 12-hour stare. This is a sly glimpse into Mexico's national pride.

ABOVE

Still from 'Osmosis and Excess' (2005)
The outskirts of Tijuana, littered with wrecked cars stripped of useful components after being brought across from the United States, is contrasted with a pharmacy in downtown San Diego, representing the vast quantities of low-cost pharmaceuticals that are smuggled from Mexico into the United States. This is part of a commodity cycle that is virtually impossible to grasp in its entirety.

TOP

Still from 'Refraction' (2005)
Designed to be a cryptic portrait of the social body as it responds to a major disaster, for this film the Dutch artist Aernout Mik recreated a major traffic accident on a rural roadway and carefully documented its cleanup.

Stills from 'Algonquin Park, September' (2001)
London-based Mark Lewis explored the
landscape genre by using a single roll of 35mm
CinemaScope film to capture the view of a misty,
frozen lake. The result is as seductive as a
classical painting.

! you don't have to put the images together into a story !

OPPOSITE TOP
Still from 'House with Pool' (2004)
Working with high-definition video, the American/
Swiss team of Teresa Hubbard and Alexander
Birchler are masters at creating entire scenarios
out of small, psychologically charged moments.
Here they place two characters in a suburban
home, a woman and a young girl, and follow
them as they wordlessly interact with the space.
No attempt is made to explain whether they are
related or not, or why they're there. Thus the
viewer enters into a dreamy filmic mystery.

OPPOSITE BOTTOM
Still from 'Single Wide' (2002)
For this video, Hubbard/Birchler used an
elaborate tracking shot and an odd scenario
involving a woman, a trailer, and a pickup truck.
The scene is viewed through the lens of a
carefully choreographed Steadicam shot, which
explores the location, the woman's presence,
and her final act of destroying the trailer with
her truck.

ABOVE
Still from 'Eight' (2001)
Being an endless loop, Hubbard/Birchler's title
refers to infinity as much as to the age of their
central protagonist, an eight-year-old girl. Here
the filmmakers follow the young girl's subjective
state as she inhabits her bedroom during a
rainstorm, passing through architectural sets
until she ventures out to salvage a bit of birthday
cake. Thus a sense of interior and exterior,
before and after, are interlaced.

*"One does not create by adding, but by
taking away. To develop is another matter."*
Robert Bresson

Mouchette (1967)

The films of Robert Bresson are unique in that they deliberately announce
themselves as artifice, and yet they achieve an unusually intense psychological
realism. Here drama is stripped down to its essential elements to introduce space,
gaps, and *temps mort*, in which the viewer projects his or her own emotions. "The
poetry," said the director, "comes from the tautness. It is not 'poetic' poetry, but a
cinematographic poetry. It arises out of simplification, which is only a more direct
way of seeing people and things."

Like many of Bresson's films, *Mouchette* (1967) tells a small story of the poor
and the disenfranchised achieving a state of grace through intense physical and
emotional hardships. But its effects are achieved almost entirely through what is
not said. The lead character is Mouchette, the eldest daughter of an impoverished,
dysfunctional family. Her mother spends the entire time in bed suffering from a fatal
illness, while her father and brother—both of whom are petty criminals and drunks—
seem incapable of any emotional, ethical, or intellectual support. As bad as things
are, Mouchette remains impassive and detached, at least until she is raped by a
local drunkard, Arsène, who is on the run, believing he killed the game warden in a

drunken stupor. That, combined with her mother's death on the same night, pushes her deeper into despair, until finally, after a family friend denounces her, saying that she was never worthy of her mother's love, and she is publicly humiliated by a local shopgirl, she takes her own life. "Mouchette offers evidence of misery and cruelty," explained the director after the film's release. "She is found everywhere: wars, concentration camps, tortures, and assassinations."

Indeed *Mouchette* is, first and foremost, a record of damnation in the Tolstoyan sense, a purely unsentimental depiction of apathy. But Bresson purposefully removed any hints at psychology, interiority, and projections of intent that were in Georges Bernanos's original novel, and focused the film entirely on banal, yet pivotal, moments in Mouchette's life. What is more, he deliberately "flattened" the image, as he was often fond of saying, by using a 50mm lens exclusively and forcing his actors through an average of 20 takes per shot. In doing so, he reduced the dialogue to empty words, which further isolates the characters in their own tragic isolation. As Jean-Pierre Améris says, "Everything radiates from the frame and into the frame in a Bresson film. So there is no need for countershots because it's all within the frame."

ABOVE
Still from 'Pickpocket' (1959)
Bresson follows an introverted Parisian who resorts to stealing as a way to cope with his pent-up anger over the death of his mother and his inability to communicate with others.

Structuralism and the Conceptual Film

The structuralist film represents a specific period in time, namely the late 1960s and 1970s, yet its influence was pervasive and it undoubtedly produced some of the most powerful and complex viewing experiences in the history of the medium.

Structuralism basically entails the process of reducing a film down to its inherent properties (structures), which in turn generates the film's content. In that sense, one can find protostructuralist work as early as the 1900s, when the futurists began to use multiple mediums, including film, in a wholly materialistic, reductive way. The short, nonnarrative film *Vita futurista* (1916) by Arnaldo Ginna is little more than a "discussion" between a pair of boxing gloves. And Robert Breer, Maya Deren, and, to a lesser extent, the film artists at the Bauhaus (most notably László Moholy-Nagy) have been cited as being protostructuralists for their often rigorous innovations with form in the 1940s and 1950s.

Nonetheless, most historians tend to agree that the Austrian avant-garde of the mid-1950s developed theories that were very much in keeping with what would later become known as structuralist filmmaking. As Steve Anker writes, Peter Kubelka, Kurt Kren, Ferry Radax, Ernst Schmidt Jr., and others "denied absolutely any conventions of their medium by restructuring the basic illusion of recorded-image-as-reality, unraveling narrative expectations and undermining the trusted value of documentation. They all directly embrace the sensual (and sometimes the taboo) through disarming formal strategies and through image content."

In other words, theirs was a rigorous formalism, initially born of modernist beliefs in releasing film from its representational function and allowing it to find—and speak—its own language. Kubelka pioneered a purely mathematical approach to editing in his groundbreaking *Adebar* (1957), where every sequence and phase becomes a multiple of the film's basic unit: 26 frames. Similarly, Kren composed his own impressionistic, almost percussive, cinematic approach, where the editing serves the content as much as the image. His landscape film, *31/75: Asyl* (*31/75: Asylum*, 1975), breaks a pastoral landscape into small squares and records each with a preplanned series of frame bursts over 21 days. Yet the final image becomes an impressionist view of pure simultaneity.

As that idea crossed the Atlantic and made it to American shores, it coincided with a period of intense renegotiation with both minimalism and modernism. For if those movements reduced the art object to a self-contained, independent, "less

ABOVE AND TOP
Stills from 'Wavelength' (1967)
One of the key films of the 1960s, Michael Snow's *Wavelength* oscillates between narrative and documentary, depth and flatness, illusion and materiality, movement and stasis. Thus, over the course of a continuous 45-minute zoom, the film evolves from the image/illusion of a room to a 2-D image of the infinite.

OPPOSITE
Still from 'The Whirlpool' (1997)
An important figure in the post-structuralist movement in the UK, Jayne Parker explores the idea of relative cinematic time by choreographing a dance underwater.

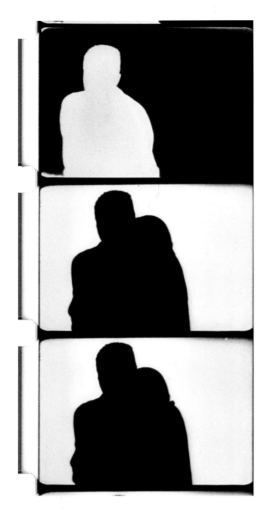

Film Strip from 'Adebar' (1957)

Arguably Peter Kubelka's most enjoyable "metric" film, *Adebar* places positive and negative shots of dancers into precise, balanced measurements. Thus, without having to rely on the actions taking place in front of the camera, he achieves a genuine sense of lyricism through the material itself.

"It is not between shots that creates the articulation of cinema, but between frames. That's where cinema speaks."

Peter Kubelka

is more" philosophy, where the basic shape evokes both organic forms and gestalt responses, American artists were attempting to go further, where the object would literally dematerialize. For them, art was meant to emphasize information systems and the social matrix rather than specific aesthetic notions of beauty. Less was still more, but, as Robert Huot said, "it wasn't enough."

In 1969 P. Adams Sitney coined the term *structural film* to describe this new wave of American filmmaking. (But his term should not be confused with linguistic or anthropological structuralism as defined by Louis Althusser or Claude Lévi-Strauss.) "Suddenly a cinema of structure has emerged," he wrote in a controversial article in *Film Culture*, "wherein the shape of the whole film is predetermined and simplified, and it is that shape, which is the primal impression of the film."

The Canadian-born, New York–based Michael Snow, in particular, earned a venerable reputation for creating entire films out of individual filmic techniques, such as the pan, the zoom, and the tilt. His most famous work, *Wavelength* (1967), appears to be a single, uninterrupted zoom from the back of a New York loft to the front, where it comes to rest on a photograph of the ocean. Thus the film takes the viewer on a journey through celluloid itself, starting with perspective views of a box (the studio) and ending with a flat image of the infinite (the ocean). But Snow didn't just stop there. He applied similar strategies to each and every element of the film: from an oblique narrative (a couple's happiness is overshadowed by a death) to temporal modes (day becomes night, past becomes present); from the color scheme (reds to greens) to the soundtrack (a 50-clicks-per-second hum to a 12,000 c.p.s. hum). As Snow says of the latter, "the sound creates a glissando while the images produce a crescendo," and the film exists somewhere in between.

Since then, Snow has continued to make works of art—in all visual mediums, including film and video—that operate through a tangible dialectic. They range from the pioneering doubled-sided projection of *Two Sides to Every Story* (1974) to the linguistic games of *"Rameau's Nephew" by Diderot (Thanx to Dennis Young) by Wilma Schoen* (1974), and from the slapstick humor of *So Is This* (1982) to the digital effects of **Corpus Callosum* (2002). In each case, the film's "engine" is the oscillation that occurs between the film's basic elements, which are generally polar extremes, such as figuration vs. abstraction, illusion vs. actuality, fiction vs. nonfiction. "I like works that keep making themselves," explains Snow, "a filmed space becomes a flat space, which becomes a strip of film, which becomes film space and back again."

Many of Snow's American peers of the late 1960s and 1970s shared similar interests, most notably Paul Sharits, Ernie Gehr, Standish Lawder, Ken Knowlton, David Rimmer, and, to a lesser extent, Andy Warhol, to name a few. For them, the goal was twofold: On the one hand, they wanted to make the perceptual process the subject of their films by emphasizing the medium's material form; and, on the other, they wanted to make films that transformed thought into pure, tangible pieces of sculpture. "I wish to abandon imitation and illusion and enter directly into the higher drama of celluloid," said Sharits, who was one of the most aggressive reductionists. "And given the fact of retinal inertia and the flickering shutter mechanism of film projection, one may generate virtual forms, create actual motion (rather than illustrate it), build color space (rather than picture it), and be involved in actual time and immediate presence."

Trained as a painter, and mentored by Stan Brakhage in Denver, Sharits was a pioneer in both installation practices and realizing the filmic equivalent of overtones—the painterly technique of using colors in a contrapuntal way, where they seem to vibrate off the canvas. His *T,O,U,C,H,I,N,G* (1968), which is spelled in such a way that it alludes to a film strip, where the letters can be read as single frames marked by sprocket holes, is a film that intercuts a half-dozen images with flashing fields of color. These frozen images—hands clawing at a face, scissors at a man's tongue, an eye surgery, and sexual penetration—are visual metaphors for Sharits's desire to quite literally penetrate through the eyes and induce a kind of transcendent state. And indeed, when viewed in the proper setting, the rapid, pulsating flicker effect creates a violent subliminal barrage that seems to connect directly to the viewer's nervous system. What is more, Sharits loops the word *destroy* on two channels of the soundtrack, which remains recognizable when the two tracks are in sync. But as the track slowly moves out of phase the word morphs into its auditory equivalent: "this drug." As Stephen Dwoskin writes, "to define the film by setting

BELOW LEFT
Film Strip from 'Leda mit dem Schwan (Materialaktion Otto Mühl)' (1964)
Using quick single-frame bursts, Austrian artist Kurt Kren successfully conveys the wildly gestural, improvised performances by the Viennese Actionists of the 1960s. Here, in a performance piece directed by Otto Mühl, a nude is exposed to fluids and paints.

BELOW
Film strip from 'Mama und Papa (Materialaktion Otto Mühl)' (1964)
In another "action" performance by Mühl involving male and female nudes, Kren creates an intensely percussive affair using a similar technique.

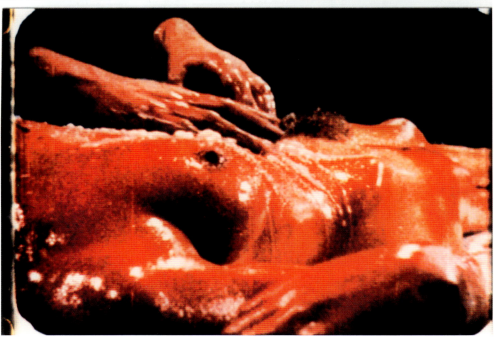

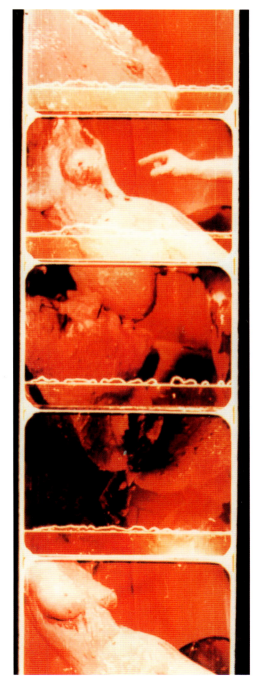

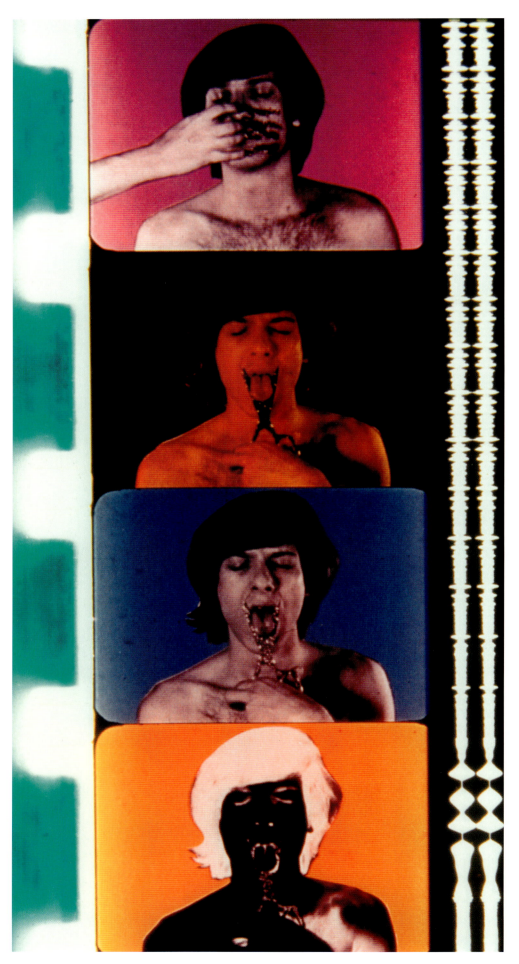

Film Strip from 'T,O,U,C,H,I,N,G' (1968)
Dedicated to, and starring, poet David Franks, this film by New York's Paul Sharits combines individual frames of solid colors with flashes of colorized static images (each showing a form of penetration, such as an eye surgery, cutting a tongue, and sexual intercourse). In the process, he creates an intense flickering effect that ultimately becomes a hypnotic visual attack.

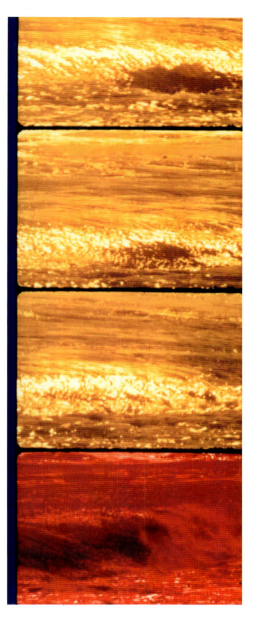

Film Strip from 'Table' (1976)

Two slightly different shots of the same table are juxtaposed in rapid succession and combined with filters. The result of Ernie Gehr's film is an intense flickering effect that seems to induce a kind of cinematic cubism.

Film Strip from 'Zorns Lemma' (1970)

With a deep interest in mathematics and language, New York's Hollis Frampton created a dry, yet intriguing, intellectual experiment, where a series of street signs are combined with shots of human actions that never come to completion. Thus the viewer is compelled to explore the nature of ordering, mathematics, and the referent.

Film Strip from 'Maxwell's Demon' (1968)

With a reference to James Clerk Maxwell, the father of both thermodynamics and the analytical theory of color, Frampton's film marries colored shots of the ocean with figures exerting energy in concise measurements.

"*The most striking break that the* cinema of structure *makes with the previous generation is in the repudiation of psychology in favor of epistemology.*"

Hollis Frampton

Still from 'Institutional Quality' (1969)
Constructed around found audio of a woman
giving a test for comprehension, Owen Land's
short work allows the viewer to follow along and
take a test. Yet Land deliberately frustrates the
process by becoming more detached as the film
progresses.

Still from 'Oh Dem Watermelons' (1965)
Originally designed to play during the
intermission of an irreverent minstrel show,
Robert Nelson's short uses a propulsive
soundtrack by Steve Reich and an array of
staged vignettes and cut-out animation to
mock racial stereotypes.

down its structures, its plan, will not give you the sensation it arouses—which is its
real meaning."

Others went even further with the flicker film, which became its own subgenre
in the 1970s. Kubelka has been credited with making the first of its kind with *Arnulf
Rainer* (1960), and, around the same time, some of the beat poets and filmmakers
experimented with the hypnotic effects of a device they called The Dreamachine,
which was little more than a lightbulb placed inside a rotation tube with slits cut
into the side. (The viewer sits in front of it, with his eyes closed, and the flickering
light patterns are said to stimulate the optic nerve and slow down brain waves
from beta to alpha and then delta.) Yet Tony Conrad's *The Flicker* (1965) remains
a benchmark of the genre. It uses 47 different flicker patterns of alternating black
and white frames, starting with a high flicker rate of 24 flashes per second and
progressing toward slower rates ranging from 18 to four frames per second. As
Conrad, who studied mathematics at Harvard, and was a member of La Monte
Young's early musical ensembles, explains the effect, "most viewers will experience
a programmed gamut of hallucinatory color effects through the intermediary of
rhythm."

By decade's end, most filmmakers had removed kinesthesia entirely from their
films (which was ultimately disparaged as decoration), and opted instead for a more
conceptual practice. New York's Hollis Frampton was an exceptionally influential
filmmaker who routinely augmented his filmmaking practice with extensive essays,
theories, and public lectures. His interest lies not so much in cinema, but in creating
a fully interdisciplinary medium that bridges filmmaking with mathematics,
linguistics, optics, and more. His *Zorns Lemma* (1970) attempts to use set theory
as a central organizational principle so that it generates a series of semipredictable
outcomes. A series of repeating street signs (from storefronts to street signage) are
slowly, and methodically, replaced with human actions, such as walking down the
street or painting a wall. Despite being somewhat dry, the significance of the film
is that its content is generated entirely through formulas and patterns. Similarly,

Hapax Legomena (1971–1972), which is one of the first films to be conceived as a complete cycle, is arranged so that its inherent parts, or individual films, are used to explore an entire range of cinematic languages that coalesce into a singular construction.

Yet Frampton was hardly alone. Many of his peers in the 1960s and 1970s, including Owen Land (aka George Landow), Ken Jacobs, Nancy Holt, Werner Nekes, Klaus Wyborny, Alan Sondheim, and a handful of pioneering video artists such as Ken Feingold, Martha Rosler, David Hall, and Robert Cahen, believed that the cinema should be forced into a place where it would ask questions about itself—its function, its meaning, and its place in the world. "Making art where you could see what made movies tick" is how Jacobs described his own objectives.

One way to do that was to "remove chance decisions, caprice, or taste," as Sol LeWitt once famously said of his own work. By doing so, the "depersonalized" product not only reveals itself and its own properties, but *forces* the viewer into reading into the work entirely with his or her own subjective response. "All legitimate art deals with limits," said Robert Smithson. "Fraudulent art feels it has no limits."

Morgan Fisher's *Screening Room* (1968/2007) consists of a single, continuous shot that moves from outside of a theater, through the entrance, and into the screening room. (The artist insists that the film can only be shown in the same theater for which it was made.) Thus, as the camera finally turns and faces the white projection screen on film, the image suddenly "pops" from the image-of-a-screen to an *actual* screen in an instant. "The oscillation between fiction, and the reality of that fiction, is what interests me," says Fisher.

Fisher and his contemporaries Owen Land, Robert Nelson, William Wegman, Joyce Wieland, and John Smith were part of a generation of the 1970s who wanted to employ humor in their structuralist works while still laying bare the conventions of the medium. Smith's *The Girl Chewing Gum* (1976) features the voice of a domineering film director "directing" people milling about in a series of (obvious)

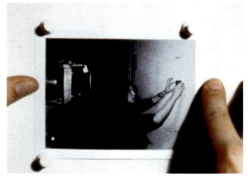

Screening Room
State for The Ahmanson Auditorium, The Museum of Contemporary Art, Los Angeles

This state may be shown only at this location. For any other screening location a corresponding state of the film must be prepared. Under no circumstances may any state of this film be broadcast on television.

ABOVE
Still from 'Production Stills' (1970)
Fisher replaces the film with a series of still photographs shot during the making of the film (production stills).

TOP
Still from 'Screening Room' (1968/2007)
California-based Morgan Fisher made two editions of this film, which can only be played in the screening room for which it was composed. Each consists of a single take beginning on the road outside the theater, entering the theater, and moving into the screen, thus fusing the image with the viewer's real-time experience.

LEFT
Still from 'The Girl Chewing Gum' (1976)
The UK's John Smith takes a seemingly random shot of a busy street in London's East End and adds his own voice-over, where he takes on the guise of a movie director trying to control the action. Thus he attempts to order around not only pedestrians, but also cars and the architecture itself.

ABOVE
Still from 'Room Film' (1973)
As a staunch anti-illusionist and a self-professed "materialist filmmaker," the UK's Peter Gidal tried to create a film that doesn't "translate or represent anything, or even [depict] consciousness," as he said. Instead the film is simply the result of light hitting celluloid.

TOP
Still from 'Crystal Aquarium' (1995)
Named after the water tanks used by stage performers in the early 1900s, Jayne Parker's film features four women—a swimmer, an ice skater, a drummer, and an observer—who perform individual actions in and around the elements. Their only connection is through rhythms.

documentary sequences to great comedic effect, especially when the director becomes increasingly despondent as his characters remain aloof and simply go about their business.

Structuralist ideas ultimately influenced commercial cinema as well in the 1970s, both in Europe and the United States. This is the period when Jean-Luc Godard, Agnès Varda, Margarethe von Trotta, Alain Tanner, John Berger, and Sally Potter brought their own self-reflexive and semiotic strategies to the narrative genre. Yet unlike experimental filmmakers who worked in a reductivist manner, these filmmakers generally attempted to emphasize the nature of signifiers (signs in and of themselves) and the signified (the nature of language and interpretation), which was, in effect, more in line with both Marxism and the actual philosophy of structuralism itself. As Godard famously said, "Art is not the reflection of reality, it is the reality of that reflection."

At the same time, there were a number of experimental filmmakers in Paris exploring their own structuralist ideas, most notably Christian Lebrat, Claudine Eizykman, and Yann Beauvais, and an even larger faction in London, with Peter Gidal, Malcolm Le Grice, Guy Sherwin, Lis Rhodes, Nicky Hamlyn, Jayne Parker, and Tony Sinden. (In fact, artists in the UK produced far more structuralist films than their American counterparts in the 1970s and 1980s, and often with greater political depth and didacticism.)

Gidal, in particular, preferred to use the Marxist term *materialist film* rather than *structuralist*, since he felt a Marxist interpretation of cinema was far more important than an aesthetic one. For him, a Marxist interpretation of cinema argues that the apparatus of the camera and the projector positions the viewer in such a way that he or she is privileged to see in a particular point of view, which means that he or she is interpolated by the filmic text. Thus the very act of watching is political, and Gidal believed that it was not only important to break the spell of the cinematic gaze, but to omit any notions of pleasure altogether. His *Denials* (1986) blurs shots of an empty room with a photograph of that same room to offer a direct challenge to Snow's *Wavelength*, which he deemed "illusionist" (and thus out to please).

Conversely, the author-filmmaker Malcolm Le Grice developed his own approach to the structuralist film, where the medium not only reveals its own plastic qualities but exposes how narratives are both artificial and arbitrary. Like David Bienstock in *Nothing Happened This Morning* (1965), he created a cinematic anagram with *Blackbird Descending (Tense Alignment)* (1977), a film that begins with an average, decidedly cliché, domestic scene between a husband and wife, but then proceeds to fold back on itself, repeating and shuffling the scene into new recombinations. (Snow recently explored similar territory with 2005's *SSHTOORRTY*, where he takes a basic narrative situation—an artist delivers one of his paintings to his lover and is confronted by her jealous husband—and edits it in such a way that it moves forward in time at the exact same rate that it moves backwards. It is an utterly mesmerizing and masterful study in temporal modes.)

A number of recent contemporary films owe an obvious debt to such experiments, including Tom Tykwer's *Lola rennt* (*Run, Lola, Run*, 1998), Christopher Nolan's *Memento* (2000), and Alejandro González Iñárritu's *21 Grams* (2003). And, more recently, a new generation of contemporary artists are exploring similar structuralist ideas, yet without the onus of the genre's narrow conventions. For many, the inspiration comes not so much from structuralism but from the possibilities of digital technologies. Marc Lafia and Didi Fire's *Variable Montage*

(2002) takes 27 frames from a Russian avant-garde film of the 1920s and combines them into five segments, each of which is associated with a small phrase from Mahler's 9th Symphony. These are then shuffled continuously via software programs without repeating once. Thus the sign, the symbol, and cinematic history are rendered arbitrary, while the code—or software program—becomes the true subject of the work.

Other artists working with similar strategies include Austrians such as Martin Arnold, Gustav Deutsch, Peter Tscherkassky, and Thomas Korschil; British and Irish artists such as Steve McQueen, Angela Bulloch, and James Coleman; and a wide array of American artists, including Gary Hill, Su Friedrich, Caspar Stracke, Konrad Steiner, Paul Sietsema, and Janis Crystal Lipzin.

Still from 'Berlin Horse' (1970)
For this film one of the UK's most important film theorists, Malcolm Le Grice, used found footage of a horse on parallel screens, which he repeated and reshot to create a lush, beautiful image that emphasizes cinematic temporalities.

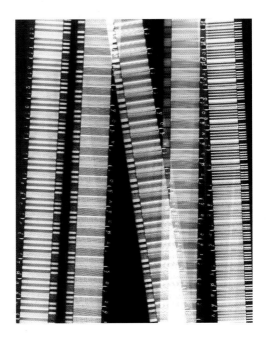

Schwechater (1958)

Peter Kubelka's name looms large in the world of avant-garde cinema. As a filmmaker, theorist, and professor with experience at dozens of universities worldwide, the Vienna-based filmmaker has inspired over three generations of artists.

His first major contribution to the art film occurred in the late 1950s, when he developed what he later called "the metric film." As Kubelka explains, "the idea is that all the elements have a relationship to the whole. So I wanted to use metric intervals in a way that's similar to music and architecture, where harmony and symmetry are essential to the overall design. But this was not a transfer of musical or architectural ideas to film, but something that comes from film itself."

Schwechater (1958) was constructed with a specific mathematical plan, which in turn produces a deliberate filmic meter and rhythmic articulation. The film was initiated after a well-known Austrian beer company by the same name invited the filmmaker to produce a 60-second spot for theatrical release. Kubelka then shot all the requisite scenes of beautiful models sipping the beverage in elegant surrounds, and then spent a year developing a visual "score" for the film, where individual frames are articulated in the manner of musical notation. For example, he used sequences composed of two black frames followed by two images, four black frames followed by four images, eight followed by eight, 16 by 16, and then down again. And each of these sequences represented different temporal moments: drinking, pouring, laughing, and the like. As a result, this 60-second film achieves a crystalline beauty, where figures freeze, fall into silhouette, hands outstretched, a face, a splash, and a movement again.

"The term *moving pictures* is a misnomer," says Kubelka. "In truth a film is composed entirely of frozen images running at 24 frames per second. And I always felt that this is where the *true* energy of cinema lies."

Of course the beer company responded with complete shock and revulsion. "It was a big scandal," confesses the filmmaker. "They put lawyers on me and I had to leave the country for some time."

Since then, Kubelka has moved into what he calls a metaphoric cycle of film-making, where metaphors between images, sounds, and ideas are used to generate new alchemical revelations. What is more, he continues to display his metric films as photographic assemblages, where the film's celluloid is mounted in adjoining strips and hung on the wall much like fine-art objects. "This is a very important aspect to my metric films," explains Kubelka.

"In a Greek temple there are pillars, which are all equally long, equally thick, and equidistant. You get the feeling of harmony. It is the same in music and [it can also be] the same in film."

Peter Kubelka

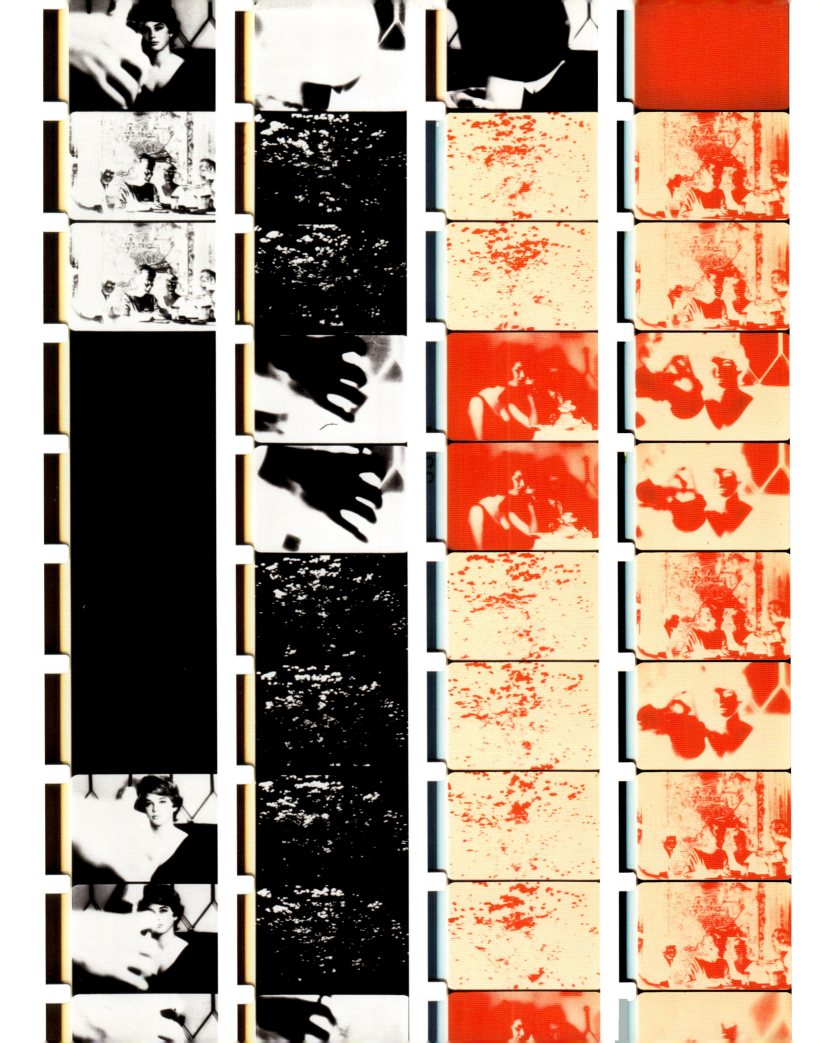

Expanded Cinema
and the Installation Film

Expanded cinema, as the term suggests, refers to a cinema that extends beyond a single projection, meaning it can consist of multiple projections in, and outside of, theaters. This is one of the most kinetic forms of filmmaking, where multiple projections, screens, and images work together not only to overwhelm the viewer, but to limn a course through collage, abstraction, performance, and the lyrical film.

While expanded cinema technically goes back to the silent era with the multiple-screen work of France's Abel Gance, its true flowering occurred in the 1960s. No single artist or artwork can claim credit for its birth. Rather, it is the result of a convergence of ideas and experiments that occurred simultaneously around the world. There was multiscreen work in Austria, France, Germany, Czechoslovakia, Japan, and the United States in the early to mid-1960s, and it was all considered performative and "expanded" filmmaking.

Nonetheless, the genre gained a considerable boost through its connection to the pop-art happenings of the late 1950s. By definition, happenings were an attempt to activate the space around an artwork, which in turn transformed the very act of viewing into a creative act. The futurists, the surrealists, and the lettristes all promoted the blurring of art and real life in the early part of the 20th Century, but the action painters of the 1940s and 1950s gave the idea its greatest currency. For them, art was not about a finished product, but a lived experience—all-consuming and immediate. That idea took on new relevance in the heated political milieu of 1960s, when the barriers between disciplines disintegrated even further. In the process a new generation of film artists—from Robert Whitman to Peter Weibel, Ken Jacobs to Carolee Schneemann, Wolf Vostell to Nam June Paik—began to see the theater as an antiquated venue belonging to Victorian times. In its place grew site-specific, one-of-a-kind events that were filled with props, projected images, and often strangely unsettling tableaux vivants. "Aimless aesthetic actions looking surreal but not really," is how Ken Jacobs described his own happenings. "The quotidian with sensibilities turned on."

At this point the projector becomes an artistic tool in its own right, which can, when directed at specific objects or locations, produce new readings of great psychological and ideological import. Robert Whitman, in particular, was known for his provoking, often humorous, projection pieces in the 1960s, which were

Installation view of 'Under Scan, Relational Architecture 11' (2005)
Upon stopping anywhere in a public square, a spectator will see in his or her shadow a figure that will begin interacting with him or her. But once the spectator moves, the figure will disappear until the spectator stops somewhere else. At that point, another figure will appear with a different set of interactions. That's the experience spectators had when walking into Rafael Lozano-Hemmer's public artwork in Trafalgar Square. It was the result of military tracking devices, over 1,000 individual video portraits, and 20 robotic projectors placed on a grid overhead.

"[By projecting onto] an architectural landmark it suddenly becomes human. Regardless of how critical we may choose to be, we have a psychological affair with these civic structures. We invest our hopes and desires. Buildings are conceived to have this effect."

Krzysztof Wodiczko

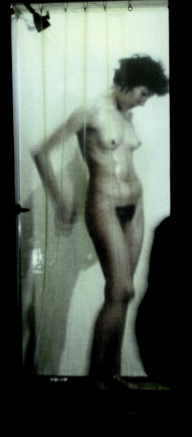

Installation views of 'Shower' (1964) Exhibition at Museu d'Art Contemporani de Barcelona, 2006
A seminal installation piece by artist Robert Whitman uses a projection of a woman bathing on an actual working shower.

born out of his interest in depth psychology. His *Shower* (1964) featured a working shower, onto which he projected the image of a nude woman bathing herself. As Mekas recalls, "The whole thing is so beautiful and so real that people kept coming back and peeking into the shower box to see if the girl was really there."

At the same time, the Austrian and British avant-gardes brought a more conceptual approach to expanded cinema in the 1960s and 1970s, respectively, and since then a wide range of artists have explored the technique to different ends, including Italy's Fabio Mauri, France's Alain Fleischer, Mexico's Rafael Lozano-Hemmer, Poland's Piotr Wyrzykowski, and America's Jennifer Steinkamp, Shelley Eshkar, and Paul Kaiser.

For many the projection of an image onto a tangible object not only dematerializes that object, but shifts the temporal state of the moving image from the past (as in the recording of a past event) to the present (where the object asserts itself as a physical thing that exists in the same space and time as the viewer). What is more, it also transforms the projector into a sculptural object with its own individual, historic, and ideological values.

Poland's Krzysztof Wodiczko believes that projections in public arenas can foster a healthy antagonism and confrontation, which in turn leads to essential public debates. For example, in Madrid, Spain, he projected images of machine guns and

gas pumps onto a triumphal arch that had been erected by the fascist General Franco. "[It is] a symbol attack," said Wodiczko of his photo-collagist methods, "a public psychoanalytical séance, unmasking and revealing the unconscious of the building."

Others still use multiple projectors to create wholly immersive environments designed to engulf the viewer in an overwhelming barrage of sensory, real-time input. Jordan Belson and Henry Jacobs both pioneered the use of overhead projectors, film loops, and appropriated imagery at their famous Vortex concerts in the late 1950s and early 1960s, which took place inside San Francisco's planetarium. But by the mid- to late 1960s that idea began to dovetail with both rock shows and public art happenings to create a purely psychedelic experience. For these filmmakers and artists alike—most notably Stan VanDerBeek, Jeffrey Shaw, Bill Ham, the group Single Wing Turquoise Bird, Andy Warhol's Exploding Plastic Inevitable, and The Joshua Light Show—psychedelia has distinct psychological and social ramifications. Being entirely of the moment, where a team of artists creates images by reacting to the situation at hand, psychedelia serves as a social adhesive that tends to overwhelm viewers en masse, and carries the potential for a collective transcendence. Indeed, with expanded cinema, the medium moves beyond notions of theatricality and into the realm of *real* experience, ritual, and ecstasy. As Jonas Mekas argued

Installation view of '1000 Platitudes' at Linz (2003)

Using the world's most powerful image projector and an almost graffiti-style approach, Mexico's Rafael Lozano-Hemmer added single letters to buildings around Linz at night. When read together, the words, such as 'multicultural', were meant to draw attention to the facile phrases used by the media to describe the "new globalized city."

in his characteristically romantic fashion, such immersive film environments could actually lead to the "transcendence of the filmic material altogether" and achieve full "actualization" of the human mind.

The dematerialization of both the art object and the space itself also helped to define what curator Chrissie Iles has defined as the second phase of installation film (the first being the happenings of Jacobs, Robert Rauschenberg, and others). This second phase, which appeared simultaneously with both the birth of portable video cameras in the late 1960s and Cagian notions of duration, attempted to distill cinema down to little more than light itself.

Anthony McCall, Bruce Nauman, Paul Sharits, Michael Snow, and Iannis Xenakis attempted to create physical sculptures out of projected light, analog video, and, in some cases, lasers. One of the most famous is McCall's *Line Describing a Cone* (1973), which projects the image of a circle being drawn on a piece of paper through a room filled with mist. That in turn creates a "solid" shape inside the projection beam, as water particles transform the "solid line" into a conical "sculpture" that exists in real space. (That piece echoes some of the light experiments by artists such as James Turrell in the 1960s.) While simple, such wonderfully mystifying works manage to both question and embrace the nature of perception—a legacy that continues in the numerous works of video artists such as Bill Viola and Gary Hill.

Each generation, of course, produces new cinematic forms and audiences alike. Recently a number of contemporary artists have explored expanded-cinema techniques, often to engage in a dialogue with mainstream, Hollywood fare. As Iles explains, this third phase of installation can be seen as a reaction to the entertainment business and its ever-deepening impact on social institutions—from the personal to the political. "The artist's use of film in the 1990s—particularly Hollywood films," she writes, "is partly to do with wanting to engage with and perhaps influence the connective tissue film creates, and participate in a common language of communication."

OPPOSITE TOP
Installation view of 'Corpocinema' (1967)
This cinematic live performance was presented by the expanded-cinema pioneer Jeffrey Shaw and other artists in a series of open-air performances at Sigma Projects in Rotterdam in 1967. Film and slides were projected onto a transparent 3-D PVC dome, while different materials were used to fill the interior space.

ABOVE
Stan VanDerBeek standing outside his Movie-Drome (circa 1965)
For VanDerBeek, one of cinema's best-known collage artists, the Movie-Drome was designed to immerse viewers in dozens of projections simultaneously. Thus no single image existed in its own right, but as part of an overwhelming tapestry of movement and sounds.

RIGHT
Installation view of 'Line Describing a Cone' (1973)
Anthony McCall's installation piece begins with a film of a hand drawing a black circle on white paper. That translates to a white cone of light as the projection beam moves through a darkened space augmented by a continual spray of mist. Thus the beam not only becomes a sculptural object in itself but becomes the real content of the work.

This is the period when installation artists around the world—from France's Pierre Huyghe, Philippe Parreno, and Dominique Gonzalez-Foerster to the UK's Mark Lewis, Tacita Dean, and Jane and Louise Wilson; from Europe's Isabell Heimerdinger, Runa Islam, and Aernout Mik to America's Dan Graham, Matthew Buckingham, and Doug Hall—ushered in a new era of psychological engagement with both the art object and Hollywood itself. Scotland's Douglas Gordon has routinely explored the psychological nature of the cinematic image and its relationship to dualism. His *Through a Looking Glass* (1999) features the famous scene from *Taxi Driver* (1976) where Robert De Niro is rehearsing the line "It's your move" in the mirror. Here Gordon projects the scene on two opposing walls, which means the viewer is quite literally caught in between an ever-questioning illusion.

Conversely, America's Doug Aitken attempts to envelop his viewers in a filmic space defined by architectural structures and physical movement through space and time. His *The Moment* (2005) features 12 screens depicting the lives of several people seemingly trapped in their own relative isolations: a woman in her apartment, a man on the street, a gesture, stasis, an action. Here the screens are situated in an *S* pattern so that the viewer must literally slalom through the narrative, picking up bits and pieces along the way, and feeling the rhythms and sounds of the work. That

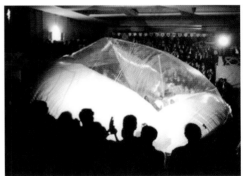

ABOVE
Installation view of 'Movie Movie' (1967)
For this multiple-projection performance at the Fourth Experimental Film Festival in Belgium, Shaw allowed the bodies of the performers and then of the audience (many of whom spontaneously took off all their clothes) to blend seamlessly with the layering of imagery.

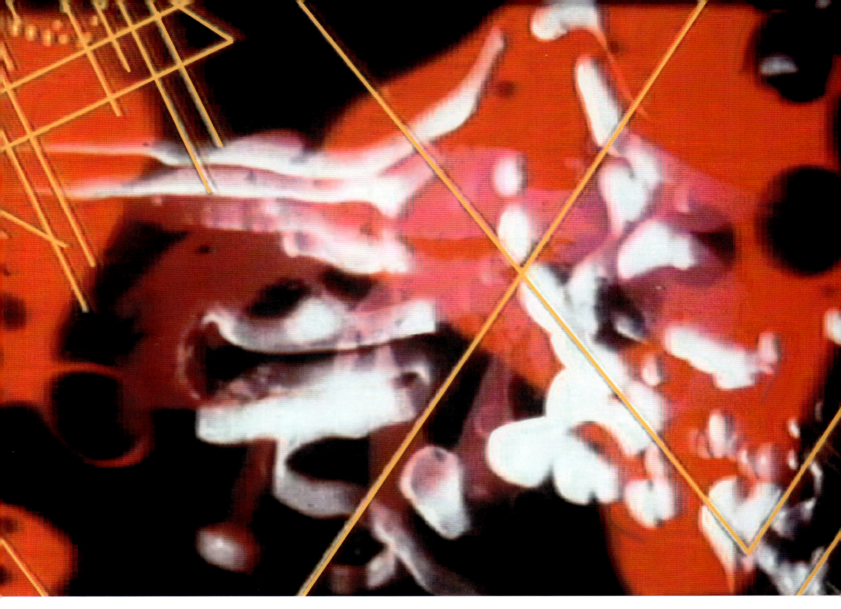

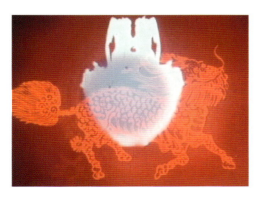

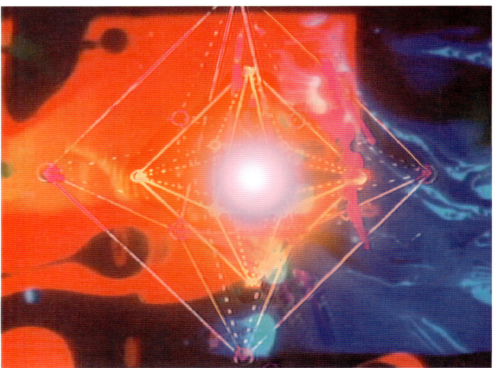

THIS PAGE & OPPOSITE
Stills from live performances by Single Wing Turquoise Bird (circa 1969)
While known for providing psychedelic visuals for musical performances, the collective Single Wing Turquoise Bird, which included Michael Scroggins, Peter Mays, Jeff Perkins, and Larry Janss, also held private performances in lofts and museums where they worked with composers such as John Cage and Terry Riley. These stills reflect a live performance from 1969, where they layered liquid, still, and moving imagery in real time, including etchings by Gustave Doré, a solar eclipse, and iconic photos of Jim Morrison.

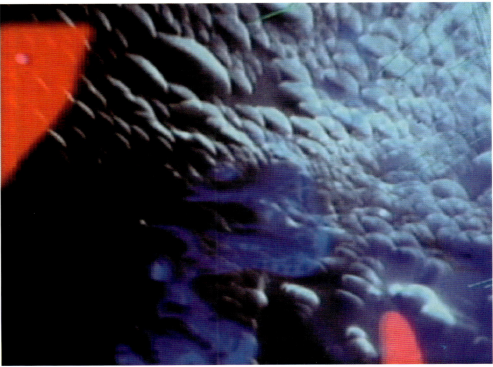

Installation view of 'The Moment' (2005)
For this installation, California's Doug Aitken used 12 plasma screens with mirrored backs and placed them in an *S* pattern in a darkened gallery. Viewers were then able to literally walk through the narrative, which follows a group of unrelated characters as they wake up each day and go about their business as if sleepwalking.

PAGES 126/127
Installation view of 'The Stopping Mind' (1991)
Using four screens, California's Bill Viola presented the viewer with simultaneous scenes of serenity, with tranquil gardens and fields of flowers. But every once in awhile, at random intervals, the four screens would burst into an instantaneous moment of absolute frenzy, and then, as if nothing happened, return to normal again.

"I don't see the narrative ending with the image on the screen. Narration can exist on a physical level, as much through the flow of electricity as through the image. Every inch of the work or of the architecture is a component of narrative."

Doug Aitken

**Installation view of 'Dispersion Room' (2005)
at Museum Ludwig, Cologne**

With this installation the Dutch artist Aernout
Mik revisits a common theme in his work—the
relationship of the individual to the group. For
this film, he orchestrated a crisis situation for a
large office tower, where workers had to conform,
take cover, and organize. But the film, which
was subsequently displayed in an actual office
setting, concentrated solely on that singular
moment of confusion.

BELOW
Installation view of 'Erewhon' (2004)

The UK's Jane and Louise Wilson are masters at
designing film and video pieces that interrogate
mute sites of power. Here they explore a decaying
sanatorium in New Zealand, where women were
forced into fitness programs as part of a post-
World War I eugenics program. Scenes were shot
at the actual site, with actors and nonactors, and
then presented in a complex series of screens
that viewers had to negotiate to see.

LEFT
Still from 'The Swan Tool' (2000–2002)
For this live performance, Berkeley-born Miranda July uses video and live music to tell the comic story of a woman who can't decide whether she wants to live or die. Instead she buries herself in her backyard.

BELOW
Still from 'Speedflesh' (1997–1998)
Using a wholly immersive environment, California artist Judith Barry created a 360-degree projection space where visitors could control the images of found and original footage floating by by turning a wheel at the center of the room.

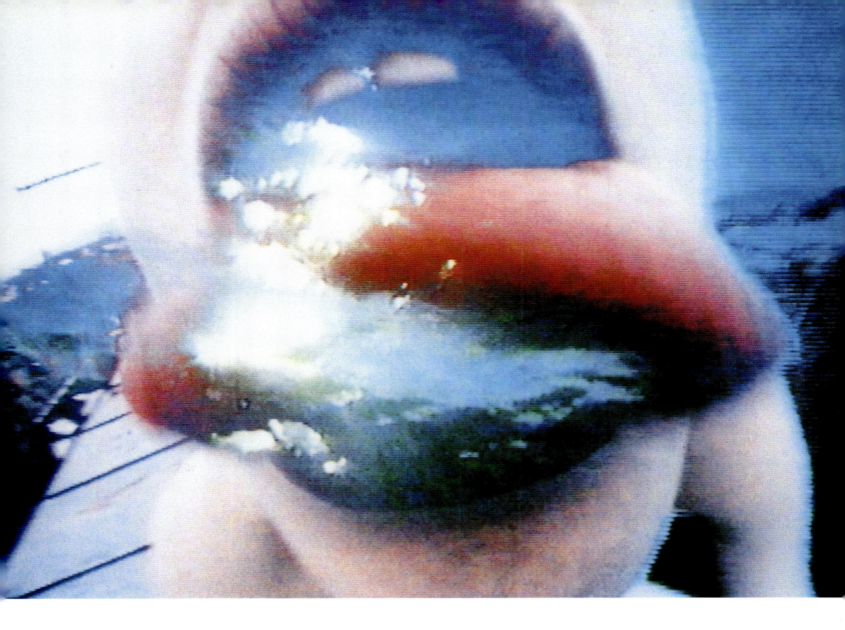

THIS PAGE
Stills from 'Pimple Porno' ('Pickelporno', 1992)
With a sensualist's interest in the body and
desire, Switzerland's Pipilotti Rist has been
searching for what she calls a nonlinguistic
mode of thought, or "the language of images,"
as she says, "which finds a more direct access
to the subconscious." For this, her breakout
video, she fuses bodyscapes with natural
landscapes to create a symphony of colorful
corporality.

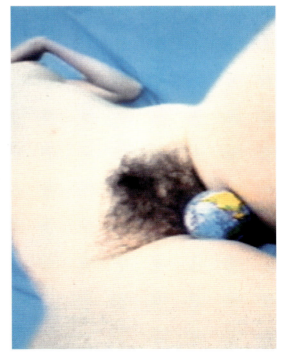

*"Film is something beyond reality. It's in
keeping with our theories about space."*
Gregory Markopoulos

**1970s set for 'Der Sandmann' (1994–1997)
at DOKFILM Studios, Potsdam 1994–1995**
Canada's Stan Douglas finds clever, overlapping
themes that connect the writings of E. T. A.
Hoffmann and Sigmund Freud, and the shared
dreams of three East Germans living under
communism, to create this landmark
installation piece.

creates a hallucinatory, almost cubist, filmic experience, where time itself seems
malleable. "The question for me is, how can I break through this idea of [temporal]
time?" asks the artist. "How can I make time somehow collapse or expand so it no
longer unfolds in this narrow form?"

Aitken is part of a new crop of "new narrative" artists that includes Pipilotti Rist,
Isaac Julien, Shirin Neshat, Eve Sussman, Jesper Just, and Anne-Mie van Kerckhoven.
For these artists, the use of projected imagery allows them to build coded
environments that reflect psychological states. As George Baker writes, this return
to a more subjective, psychological experience differs from previous generations
of installation artists in that "[the] work doesn't engage in an anti-aesthetic critique
of representation, as postmodernism did, but instead creates an aesthetic of emotion
and psychic intensities."

More recently, installation has moved into a fourth stage, which is defined by
wholly interactive mediums, where both the artist and the viewer remain in a
physical relationship with the work, which in turn defines the subject matter. These
artists—Jeffrey Shaw, Liisa Roberts, Judith Barry, Lynn Hershman Leeson, Caspar
Stracke, Janet Cardiff and George Bures Miller, Jennifer and Kevin McCoy, and
the collective Blast Theory—are less interested in creating traditional "canned"
experiences, where the work always remains the same, than in creating wholly

open-ended works that remain forever in flux—much like life itself. For critic Ross Gibson, that suggests a radical paradigm shift, where people will look to the arts to quite literally "be differently in themselves."

Der Sandmann (1995)

When it debuted in 1997, Stan Douglas's *Der Sandmann* (1995) was immediately hailed as one of the most significant artworks of the 1990s, and rightly so. It is a complex, thought-provoking work of art that remains a benchmark for film installation.

It consists of a stage set that resembles a small storybook house, fully furnished, with a small garden and faux landscape outside the front door. Next to that is a large screen that projects a continuous, 360-degree pan from inside the same house—a pan that is bifurcated down the middle so that it reflects both past and present at once. In other words, as the pan moves from left to right, it continually wipes out the "historical" image with the newer one. For Douglas, that idea touches on Nietzsche's theory of eternal recurrence, where everything is doomed to repeat itself endlessly. But the work achieves even greater complexity by virtue of three interrelated voice-overs, which explore Freud's essay "The Uncanny," social theory, and E. T. A. Hoffmann's dream story, *Der Sandmann* (1816).

"The intent," said Douglas, who is based in Vancouver, "is to evoke certain historical moments and certain notions of absence."

And since then, Douglas has continued to explore failed utopias, the split self, and various machines that can, and do, remake themselves over and over again. His *Journey into Fear* (2001) continually reshuffles short dialogues between characters on a container vessel at sea so that it can run for 157 hours without repeating itself. Thus, as visitors enter at different times, they are each guaranteed to have a unique cinematic experience.

ABOVE AND TOP
Stills from 'Horror Chase' (2002)
This interactive environment by Jennifer and Kevin McCoy randomly samples chase scenes from Sam Raimi's *Evil Dead 2* and places the viewer squarely at the center of what seems to be a moment of never-ending panic.

LEFT
Still from 'Der Sandmann' (1995)
Projected on a screen placed inside Stan Douglas's installation, this single image consists of two simultaneous 360-degree pans that overlap at the center. One side shows a postwar landscape, and the other shows the same in the present. Thus the present continuously wipes out the past.

"The problem of film lies essentially in the articulation of time and only very secondarily in the articulation of form."

Hans Richter

Collage and the Found-Footage Film

Both Dada and surrealist filmmakers exploited the alchemical effects of juxtaposition in both literary and visual works of art. With the rise of new sociopolitical battles in the 1950s it became the prevailing aesthetic of the period, precisely because it reflected the times better than most other contemporary-art practices. As poet Robert Creeley described the era, "There seemed to be no logic, so to speak, that could bring together all the violent disparities of [the chaos of world war]. The arts especially were shaken and the picture of the world that might previously have served them had to be reformed."

Further fueled by the ideas of Jean-Paul Sartre, John Cage, Werner Heisenberg, Karl Marx, and Albert Einstein, which utterly destroyed any notion of permanence, this was the period when collage, assemblage, and found art left its mark on virtually every aspect of the avant-garde. Jean-Luc Godard and the French New Wave responded in kind by introducing a more disjointed, improvisatory style of juxtaposition into mainstream filmmaking. But the beat filmmakers of the same period—Christopher Maclaine, Antony Balch, and Conrad Rooks—went even further in exploring chance accidents, counterpoint, and sheer randomness.

Yet the very notion of collage is somewhat problematic for cinema since film is by nature a time-based medium that can only present shots in sequence as opposed to all at once. Both Robert Breer and Paul Sharits tried to confront that idea in their own films, where they attempted to present subjects simultaneously, much like in a painting. But for most critics, the animated photo assemblage was, and still is, the purest form of film collage.

Harry Smith helped to define the genre in the 1950s when he began to incorporate surrealist techniques of automatism and juxtaposition into his handmade photo collages. Similarly, Robert Breer, Stan VanDerBeek, and Lawrence Jordan pulled images from magazines, books, and other printed material to create mesmerizing, often hilarious, collages of the 1950s and 1960s. Since then Victor Faccinto, Lewis Klahr, Nancy Edell, Janie Geiser, and Marcel Dzama have followed suit with equal success.

But if collage can be defined as a process of using real, found objects in the picture plane (à la Picasso), one could argue that the found-footage film, where preexisting material is appropriated and transformed through montage and juxtaposition, is the cinema's equivalent.

Still from 'Viet-Flakes' (1965)
Carolee Schneemann's pioneering film and video work has always dealt with the body and its relationship to social mores, conventions, and politics. Here she appropriates male-oriented images of war atrocities from Vietnam to create a fever dream of multiple exposures, which in turn suggests a deeply personal take on a national trauma.

"Just putting images together, relationships between things are suggested … A large part of the construction of almost any communication has to be the recreation by the person who experiences it. Then there's the space between the images also, which is also important."

Bruce Conner

ABOVE
Production still from 'Pierrot le fou' (1965)
For France's Jean-Luc Godard, pictured above, this film was an attempt to explore the clash of idealisms coursing through the 1960s, both in the public sphere and in cinema. Thus he blends the romanticism of the road film with dozens of pop-cultural references, film styles, and literary motifs.

OPPOSITE TOP
Still from 'Contempt' ('Le Mépris', 1963)
One of a number of films where Godard explores the nature of the creative process as it relates to cinema. Here Jack Palance (left) plays an uncultured American producer who forces his screenwriter, played by Michel Piccoli, to rethink Homer's *Odyssey*, while trying to seduce his wife, played by Brigitte Bardot.

Found-footage filmmaking dates back to the 1920s and 1930s, when Esfir Shub made *Padenie dinastii Romanovykh* (*The Fall of the Romanov Dynasty*, 1927) and Joseph Cornell made *Rose Hobart* (1936). These two films showed that one could tease out entirely new meanings from material that was either discarded or shot for other purposes. A generation later, the American sculptor Bruce Conner brought significant attention to the genre with his first effort, *A Movie* (1958), which creates a genuinely affecting mood through precise rhythms and ingenious couplings. Here a morbid display of mass destruction culled from documentaries, Hollywood adventure fare, and stag films achieves a certain level of black humor, which belies Conner's beat ethos. Yet at the same time, it continually exhibits an extraordinary sense of rhythm, which is enhanced by the repeated use of self-reflexive material such as countdown leader, intertitles, and credit sequences.

That film solidified Conner's reputation as a master of ironic counterpoint despite the fact that his later work changed significantly in tone and approach. (*Crossroads* [1976], *Take the 5:10 to Dreamland* [1977], and the autobiographical *Valse Triste* [1977] trade contrast for a more lyrical aesthetic, where images are celebrated as much as they are debased.) As a result, he inspired over three generations of filmmakers, including Arthur Lipsett in the United States, Maurice Lemaître in France, and Giorgio Turi and Gianfranco Baruchello in Italy. The latter made a

BOTTOM LEFT
Still from 'The End' (1953)
San Franciscan beat poet Christopher Maclaine gained notice for this highly expressive film, which consists of several loose-knit portraits of people on the last days of their lives.

BOTTOM RIGHT
Still from 'Scotch Hop' (1959)
Maclaine intercuts scenes of bagpipers with seemingly random shots of costumed women to create a collage film that ultimately defies easy interpretations.

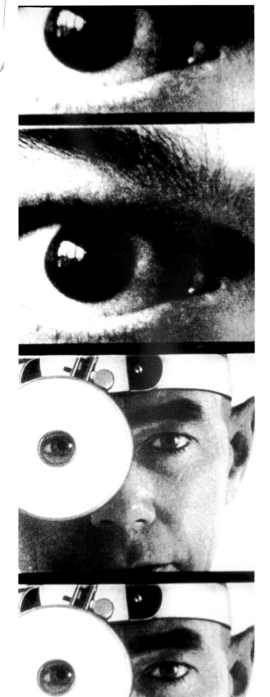

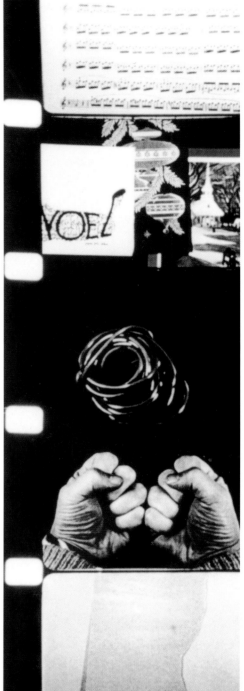

RIGHT
Film strip from 'A La Mode' (1957)
Inspired by Dada and the beat movement, New York's Stan VanDerBeek produced dozens of irreverent, humorous cut-out animations in the 1960s that gained notice for their political iconoclasm. Here he riffs on pop culture by using imagery culled from 1950s fashion advertisements.

FAR RIGHT
Film strip from 'Recreation' (1956)
Michigan-born Robert Breer is a key figure in the experimental-film scene, primarily for his ability to explore cinema in the way that painters might approach a canvas. With this film he puns on the word *recreation* by giving one frame of film to thousands of common objects. The result is a percussive, highly impressionistic view that has often been compared to beat poetry.

OPPOSITE BOTTOM
Still from 'The Visual Compendium' (1991)
Using found graphics from the turn of the century and vintage steel engravings, Denver-born Larry Jordan emerged in the 1970s as one of the most accomplished collage filmmakers in the world. For this 17-minute film, which took 2½ years to make, he strung together a series of vaguely related, surreal moments to create a seamless adventure into the subconscious.

number of caustic yet humorous found-footage films that circulated widely through festivals in the 1960s, including *La Verifica Incerta* (1964), a hilarious collage film made entirely out of hackneyed Hollywood westerns and period epics.

The postmodern milieu of the 1970s and 1980s inspired a new era of image appropriation, which in turn influenced collage filmmakers. That is when an untold number of artists—from Saul Levine to Peggy Ahwesh; Craig Baldwin to Keith Sanborn; Mañuel DeLanda to Dietmar Brehm—began to push filmic collage into new directions. Terry Cannon's surrealist exercise *A Show for the Eyes* (1981) used a mail-art approach, where filmmakers from around the world (James Broughton, Michael Hoolboom, Jeff Poe, and others) donated short pieces of film that were pieced together as they arrived. Leslie Thornton's *Peggy and Fred in Hell* (1985–present), on the other hand, uses a cross-platform collage, where the adventures of two adolescents are followed across a wide spectrum of found-footage films, videos, art pieces, and installation works that are designed to work en masse.

Meanwhile, a number of avant-garde artists working in the 1990s reexplored themes of psychological engagement, often making entirely new fictions of great psychological import out of preexisting material. Jay Rosenblatt's *Short of Breath* (1990) uses vintage 1950s educational films to develop a fictional story about a boy who literally absorbs his mother's depression and becomes a depressive himself. And New York's Abigail Child made *The Future Is Behind You* (2004), a completely fictional autobiography made out of preexisting home movies from the 1930s. ("An exercise in historical immaterialism?" she asks.) Indeed, few collage filmmakers have proven to be quite as adept at nuance as the Cambridge-based Child. For the

ABOVE
Still from 'Rose Hobart' (1936)
Generally credited as being the first cinematic act of appropriation, *Rose Hobart* was born out of the scraps of a B-grade Hollywood adventure film featuring a secondary character played by the actress Rose Hobart. Artist Joseph Cornell subsequently re-edited the film to make Hobart the central figure and emphasize her subjectivity. The result was so surreal that Salvador Dalí claimed that it was the only film that he wished he had made.

LEFT AND MIDDLE
Stills from 'Take the 5:10 to Dreamland' (1977)
Contrasting his hyperkinetic style of collage, San Francisco's Bruce Conner combines seemingly random moments culled from travel films to create a gentle, dreamlike affair where small-town moments are recombined to create odd connections, subtle rhythms, and poetic revelations.

BOTTOM LEFT AND RIGHT
Stills from 'Valse Triste' (1977)
Conner uses a slower pace to suggest a dreamlike autobiography that reflects his own childhood in Kansas.

OPPOSITE
Film strips from 'Looking for Mushrooms' (1967/1996)
This is one of two versions that Conner made of the same film. The original version, shown here, features rapid-fire shots that he took while traveling through small pueblos in Mexico. The result finds uncommon rhythms and patterns in storefronts, random people, and fireworks.

"My role of being an artist, as it might be defined in our society, is to create a dialogue between myself and another person. This is a duality. The process of change in this relationship is what I'm interested in. I want other people to be a mirror image of me."

Bruce Conner

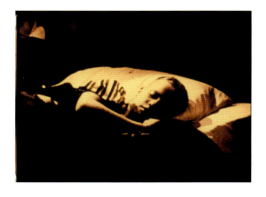

better part of the last 30 years she has been pulling whimsical moments (and outtakes) from unrecognizable feature films, documentaries, industrials, telenovelas, vintage porn, and, most importantly, home movies. Yet unlike many of her peers, she often uses prosaic, everyday moments—a smile here, a tug of the arm there—to build lyrical tapestries of pure visual poetry. The structure of her often hypnotic seven-part series, *Is This What You Were Born For?* (1981–1989), is a spiral shape, where identical images are reintroduced time and again. And with each reintroduction, the image is given a new context, thus allowing for a different, free association. "It's a rich, open structure that you keep adding and expanding," said Child. "It also allows for associations, peripheries, returns back beside itself but changed, like memory and consciousness."

Others working toward a more personal, psychological, or political register include both film artists, such as Alan Berliner, Standish Lawder, and Su Friedrich, and contemporary installation artists, such as Douglas Gordon, Johan Grimonprez, and Matthew Buckingham. Of the former group, the optical printer has eclipsed the camera as being the most important tool in the creation of an artwork. Thus, for Phil Solomon, Pat O'Neill, Peter Tscherkassky, Bill Morrison, Dietmar Brehm, and Gustav Deutsch, filmmaking is first and foremost a darkroom practice, where images are composited rather than composed.

That's also true for Ken Jacobs, who stands as an essential figure in the canon of art filmmaking. Few have explored the notion of found footage—whether it is classic Hollywood narratives, comedy, documentary film, or even his own original footage—with quite his level of purity. For him, preexisting material is not a source of imagery that can be chopped up and subverted, but living tissue that embodies history. As the Brooklyn-born filmmaker once said, "I've always enjoyed mining existing film and seeing what it remembers and what it misses."

Indeed, he sees each consecutive project as an ever-deepening celebration of celluloid—from *Tom, Tom, the Piper's Son* (1969), which is a two-hour rhapsody of a 10-minute sequence inside a pre-Griffith narrative, to *Perfect Film* (1985), an unedited collection of documentary outtakes that evolve into a haunting meditation on the way Malcolm X's assassination was (mis)handled by the media.

More recently, he has turned to "performing" with found footage in real time. His *Nervous System Performances*, in particular, use two analytical projectors to project two identical prints simultaneously onto a single screen. That allows Jacobs to manipulate the material with filters and a variable shutter speed to create a hypnotic, semiabstract film performance of great power. "These works are all very, very experiential," said Jacobs. "They're all very involved in the immediate for me."

Live cinema, which echoes the oldest form of cinema, the magic lantern, was anticipated by Jacobs and his peers, namely Tony Conrad, Malcolm Le Grice, and Guy Sherwin, as well as a number of video pioneers in the 1960s and 1970s, including Nam June Paik, John Whitney Jr., and Steve Beck. It resurfaced in the 2000s with artists such as Sue Costabile, Gregg Biermann, Julien Maire, Bradley Eros, Luis Recoder, and the collectives silt and Wet Gate. These artists are devoted to making improvisatory, liquid cinemas, where analog abstractions, miniature models, and digital projections are manipulated in real time.

A related practice is video "scratching," where an artist manipulates footage like a DJ works a turntable. Both Martin Arnold and the video artists Steina and Woody Vasulka initiated the practice in the 1980s, but in recent years Christian Marclay, Paul Pfeiffer, Piotr Wyrzykowski, Scott Stark, and Kevin Hanley have made it part of their contemporary-art practice.

Mother + Father (2005), by the South African–born, Berlin-based Candice Breitz, features a series of monitors that display individual actors culled from well-known Hollywood movies. Here Julia Roberts, Meryl Streep, Faye Dunaway, Steve Martin, Harvey Keitel, and Dustin Hoffman seem to talk to one another by the careful manipulation, or "scratching," of picture and sound. At one point Streep, who is playing a parent like the others, says that she is finally "okay" after years of therapy. To which Faye Dunaway replies, "You know, your problem is you're so self-involved!"

More recently, a number of artists have begun to use advanced software programs to define a new dawn of image appropriation, one that has distinct social, aesthetic, and political ramifications. The Canadian-based Marco Brambilla raised the bar in 2008 by using software programs that could isolate moving imagery

"In real life there are no stories. Everything is unending, confusing, nothing starts and concludes. There's no beginning, middle, and end in the total experience of our lives."
Ken Jacobs

ABOVE & TOP
Stills from 'Film Noir' (2005)
Using his own cut-out animation techniques, the UK's Osbert Parker tells an oblique narrative of film-noir characters culled from well-known movies running amok.

LEFT
Still from 'Recounting a Dancing Man' (1998)
California artist Kevin Hanley uses a four-minute segment of Fred Astaire tap dancing in *The Belle of New York* (1952) to explore a software program that samples the segment at random. Thus Astaire jerks and breaks much like a DJ "scratching" a record, which in turn creates its own original soundtrack.

ABOVE
Still from 'Peggy and Fred in Hell' (1985)
An early example of cross-medium collage by
the Rhode Island–based Leslie Thornton, where
video, film, installation, and actual objects
combine to tell a fragmented story about a pair
of teens on the run in a postapocalyptic world.

OPPOSITE
Stills from 'Short of Breath' (1990)
Despite using found footage, California's Jay
Rosenblatt manages to tell the story of a young
boy who absorbs his mother's depression while
she strives to be a good wife.

culled from popular feature films to construct composite images that combine as many as 400 layers at once. Thus, a collage effect, where all the images exist simultaneously, could be achieved much like a painting. Other key efforts include those by the New York-based Michael Joaquin Grey, who uses bits and bytes from common movies to create a form of "computational cinema," as he calls it. His *Perpetual Zooz* (2005) features *The Wizard of Oz* (1939) playing on the recto-verso sides of a rotating plane that spins endlessly in a yellow field. More importantly, he uses his own proprietary software to make the images react synaesthetically to the film's soundtrack, which means that various elements inside the picture plane—faces, body parts, props—react to certain sounds and pulsate *toward* the viewer in three dimensions, much like a topographical map, as it rotates in space. Meanwhile, each side of the rotating plane shows the film running in different directions, one forward and the other backward. As Grey explains, "I thought of [the piece] as this perpetual motion machine, which plays itself out in space as well as time, the increased surface of the film object realizing a new form of memory."

> *"Images have different weights and different values. Meaning is assigned to them at the moment of reception rather than being inherent to them in some essential way."*
>
> **Candice Breitz**

RIGHT

Stills from 'Mayhem' (1987)

New York's Abigail Child is one of the most accomplished found-footage filmmakers in the United States. Her films, which are born out of her interest in both history and literature, are the result of intensive research and a deft touch. *Mayhem*, which is part of a larger cycle of films, combines little-known noir imagery and early Japanese porn to hint at a secretive story of criminal behavior.

OPPOSITE

Film strips from 'Runs Good' (1971)

As one of the great masters of special effects, California's Pat O'Neill ran an array of original footage through a homemade optical printer to create this collage work. The title uses a common slogan found in a used-car lot to draw parallels between a car engine and a 16mm projector and mechanical reproduction and cinema itself.

PAGE 146

Multiple screens from 'Mother + Father' (2005)

By isolating close-ups from Hollywood movies (all female leads playing mothers), Germany's Candice Breitz puts each one on an individual monitor and edits them into humorous—and surprisingly cohesive—conversations. When she combines these with male figures edited in the same manner, she is able to highlight the pseudopsychology of cinematic parenting.

PAGE 147 BOTTOM

Still from 'Nervous System Performances' (1990–present)

By projecting a number of early silent comedies simultaneously with paired analytical projectors, Jacobs invented a 3-D effect that reimagines and manipulates Hollywood history with an eye toward the hidden and the repressed.

Video Quartet (2002)

"What distinguishes Christian Marclay's work from others who recombine fragments of found cultural material," explains critic Miwon Kwon, "is the extent to which the coming together of the parts remains intelligible as a structurally integral aspect of the work. That is, the seams are not smoothed over to create the illusion of a natural whole. Meaning lies in the seams."

That description summarizes Marclay's *Video Quartet* (2002) beautifully. Here a quartet of screens spanning the length of a gallery presents a collage of 700 individual clips from Hollywood films including *Casablanca* (1942), *Back to the Future* (1985), *Barbarella* (1968), *Some Like It Hot* (1959), and *This Is Spinal Tap* (1984).

Each shot is carefully orchestrated to work within the overall structure, which becomes its own found-music score. We see a shot of a man playing a banjo coupled with a shot of a woman stomping her feet. Then Jack Nicholson appears playing the piano in *Five Easy Pieces* (1970), followed by Dustin Hoffman playing vibraphone in *Midnight Cowboy* (1969). Together, these pieces create a mesmerizing, comical, yet totally improbable composition that stands on its own as a unique musical composition.

The project was born out of Marclay's long interest in both Dada-style appropriation and the discrepancy between sound and image. His *Up and Out* (1997) imprints the soundtrack to Brian De Palma's *Blow Out* (1981) over Michelangelo Antonioni's *Blowup* (1966) to create a dialectic between the two (the former being about a soundman and the latter being about a photographer). Similarly, *Gestures* (1999) uses four screens to present four views of Marclay's hands as he "scratches" turntables to create an improvisatory audio-visual composition in real time.

Those works ultimately fed into the creation of *Video Quartet*, which in turn has pushed the artist increasingly into the realm of interactivity and chance. "The music of the future will be constantly manipulated," said Marclay in 2004. "[It will] always be evolving, an unstable flow of sounds, never the same twice."

ABOVE
Installation view of 'Video Quartet' (2002)
New York's Christian Marclay carefully juxtaposes individual musical scenes culled from hundreds of Hollywood films to create a new musical composition.

BELOW
Still from 'Star Spangled to Death' (2004)
Ken Jacobs's six-hour epic is a cavalcade of found and original footage, including vintage newsreels, surreal cartoons, and his footage of New York hipsters circa 1958. Described as the "ultimate underground film," it is a lament for lost idealism.

Portraiture and Autobiography

Portraiture remains one of cinema's most popular subgenres, one that percolates throughout the entire history of both commercial and documentary film. But it is also prevalent among experimental film artists looking to explore the nature of representation in new, often exciting, ways.

The underground film communities of the 1940s, 1950s, and 1960s were particularly interested in portraiture, and they often stamped it with an expressionistic sensibility akin to the lyrical film. Marie Menken, Gregory J. Markopoulos, Ed Emshwiller, Robert Frank, Margaret Tait, Warren Sonbert, and Stephen Dwoskin have created films where the central figure is less a personhood than the site of specific feelings and impressions. Henwar Rodakiewicz anticipated such films with his *Portrait of a Young Man in Three Movements* (1931), a film that shows us nothing more than a man's personal possessions—his night table, books, clothing, and the like—without a single shot of the eponymous young man.

Scotland's Margaret Tait followed a similar approach in her portrait films of the 1960s and 1970s, which often placed equal emphasis on objects, possessions, and locations. "I suppose that [idea] is perhaps related to the way a painter would treat different things on a canvas," she once said. "To quote Lorca, 'an apple is no less intense than the sea; a bee no less astonishing than a forest.'"

One can find a similar theme running through the many portrait films of Gregory J. Markopoulos of the 1960s, which the filmmaker later assembled into a single work called *Galaxie* (1966). Taken as a whole, the project provides a glimpse into the creative scene of the era, with intimate portraits of nearly 40 well-known artists, writers, filmmakers, and poets, including W. H. Auden and Jasper Johns. For each film, Markopoulos did extensive research into the subject's life beforehand, but rarely, if ever, preplanned any shots. Instead, each film was composed intuitively, usually at the subject's house or work space, and edited entirely in-camera on a single, three-minute roll of film. Thus, the style of each film—the instantaneous frame bursts, multiple exposures, and static takes—becomes a record of his own emotional and subjective interaction with his material.

An extreme version of that idea can be seen in the more recent digital work of the late American artist Jeremy Blake, who used video synthesizers and digital software programs to transform both found and original material into deliberately psychedelic/abstract compositions. *Winchester* (2002) and *Sodium Fox* (2005) are

ABOVE
Still from 'Lovers and Lollipops' (1956)
When François Truffaut was asked for his inspiration for taking cinema out into the streets, he cited the work of Morris Engel and Ruth Orkin. Engel and Orkin, who were both still photographers, used a cinéma vérité style to tell this story of a New York model who shares an apartment with her daughter, and begins a relationship with a humble engineer.

OPPOSITE
Still from 'Trash' (1970)
Andy Warhol and director Paul Morrissey's camp classic subverts Hollywood melodrama motifs by trading movie sets for real locations, movie stars for nonactors, and drama for boredom.

"The body is a picture machine with an endless reservoir of images, feelings, and sounds."

Pipilotti Rist

149

two long-form looped works that can be seen as the psychological projections of
their subjects: California's notorious Winchester mansion, for the former, and the
poet David Berman, for the latter. In both cases, specific imagery morphs from
recognizable figures—e.g., the liquor bottles, spiderwebs, and women of *Sodium
Fox*—into psychographic landscapes of the mind. As Blake said, "I've come to see
[this process] as a kind of time-based, 21st-Century American landscape painting."

Conversely, Andy Warhol revolutionized cinematic portraiture in the 1960s by
distilling the images of his subjects down to static, real-time presentations without
any editorializing whatsoever. "The great stars," said Warhol, "are the ones who
are doing something you can watch every second, even if it's just a movement
of the eye."

While his *Sleep* (1963) was composed of edited sequences and looped shots, it
can also be seen as a relentless, 321-minute stare at one of his favorite subjects, John
Giorno. (He originally wanted Brigitte Bardot for the sleeper, although it would
have made his premise a little too obvious.) That is why critic Russell Ferguson
argues that the film solidified Warhol's concept of the "star," which is, in his words,
"about stasis—the icon only—no action required."

Such films have a legacy in much of today's installation work, where individuals
are represented on screens directly, without montage effects or commentary. Fiona
Tan shot 300 portraits of inmates and guards at a correctional facility in California
and rendered each in a three-quarter body shot à la classic Hollywood compositions.
Each stared directly into the camera for 40-second intervals, without moving. She
then projected the work, called *Correction* (2005), on six screens placed in a circle,
where the viewer could actually feel what it's like to be surrounded by both
hardened criminals and authority figures alike.

At this point the cinematic portrait blends seamlessly with the tableau, as
Warhol, Viola, and Wilson have previously illustrated. Finland's Eija-Liisa Ahtila
uses static, projected tableaux to create immersive spaces based on distinct
psychological models. For her, that allows her to explore the subject of identity—

in particular, the representation of women in the media—and how that, in turn, relates to cinematic conventions. The idea for her *If 6 Was 9* (1995) came from the experience of driving around Los Angeles and seeing Calvin Klein billboards of hypersexualized girls staring directly into the camera. For Ahtila, such images suggested a singular narrative broken up spatially across the urban environment. With that in mind, she created an installation where the viewer moves through three screens, each depicting an individual teenage girl addressing the camera directly and discussing her sexuality in frank terms. In that way the viewer encounters a fractured, but potent, reflection of three young women—the epitome of what Madison Avenue sees as ideal subjects—as they relate their own troubled thoughts.

By contrast, America's Sharon Lockhart uses a methodology much like James Benning's in her latest film, *Pine Flat* (2005), which features 12 static, tableau-style portraits of teenagers living around a small, unnamed town. Each shot lasts exactly 10 minutes, and each presents an individual or a small group locked in their own respective interiorities. We see a young boy in one segment practicing his harmonica and pacing about in a cove of rocks. And in another, two boys and a girl run through a rural landscape, chasing each other, playing, wrestling, smoking cigarettes, and

BELOW
Sequence from 'Sodium Fox' (2005)
Jeremy Blake's psychedelic brand of portraiture includes animation, found footage, and computer renderings, which are woven together to create a subjective representation of the poet David Berman.

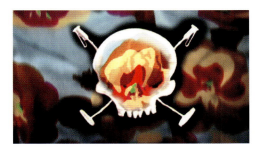

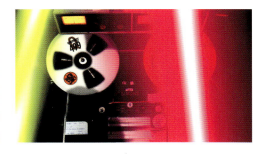

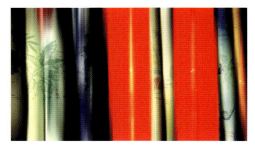

ABOVE
Installation view of 'Correction' (2005)
Picking up on Andy Warhol's *Screen Tests*, the Indonesian-born Fiona Tan presents 300 portraits of U.S. inmates and guards who stand perfectly still for 40 seconds each. Tan then presents the work in a circle to entrap the viewer.

RIGHT
Stills from 'Predictive Engineering' (1999)
Using a combination of real-time video and prerecorded material, New York–based Julia Scher transformed seven "zones" of the San Francisco Museum of Modern Art into a heightened state of video surveillance, which in turn raised critical questions about power, ideology, and control.

dodging a sudden rainfall. While Lockhart's previous takes on the city symphony, *Goshogaoka* (1997) and *Teatro Amazonas* (1999), had combined strong ethnographic and narrative impulses, the dead time of *Pine Flat* is much more Cagian in its effect. As Michael Ned Holte writes, "Lockhart is not exactly telling stories so much as finding—and constructing—a meeting place between her subjects and the imaginary their filmed presence generates."

The UK's Gillian Wearing, on the other hand, takes a more critical approach to portraiture, which often touches on the cult of celebrity and the social aspects of voyeurism. For *10–16* (1997), she recorded the voices of children confessing their deepest feelings, and then had middle-aged adults (often their parents) lip-synch to playback machines. Thus we see a nude, heavily tattooed, middle-aged dwarf sitting in a bathtub and explaining in the voice of a child how he'd like to kill his mother and her lesbian lover, the so-called big white swan. While this surreal, often humorous piece overtly plays with the idea that we never outgrow our inner child, it also plays with the notion that images tend to exist in a continuum, residing somewhere in memory, whereas sound tends to evoke the present moment.

All of these works share an interest in the socially constructed self and all its affects. Yet one can also use surveillance techniques, e.g., remote-control cameras, as an artistic strategy, which not only pushes the theme of social construction to the extreme but introduces issues of control, power, and menace.

In the 1960s and 1970s video surveillance often dealt with the reflexive nature of television and its deadening effect on viewers. Arthur Ginsberg's pioneering video *The Continuing Story of Carel and Ferd* (1970–1975) featured a live closed-circuit TV feed of two real people—an adult film actress and her bisexual junkie boyfriend, living in a small apartment—for weeks at a time. Consequently, their exploits, which included real-life domestic squabbles, drug abuse, and sexual activities, were presented on eight monitors for an audience to peruse at will. For Ginsberg, the project was designed both to show the consequences of surveillance and to lay bare the public's obsession with voyeurism.

But that idea has found new relevance in an age when computers have extended the body's capacity to exchange and enter into a wider matrix of information.

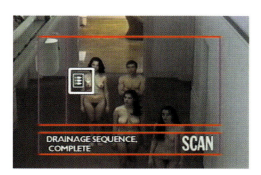

Still from 'The 4 Seasons of Veronica Read' (2002)
Turkish-born Kutluğ Ataman routinely explores portraiture by making lengthy videos that tend to outlast the viewer's attention. This four-screen installation features Veronica Read waxing poetically about her 900 Hippeastrum bulbs, which in turn becomes a self-reflexive expression of beauty, possession, and obsession.

Installation view of '31' (2002)
For this installation work, artist Lorna Simpson documented the life of a young woman over a 24-hour period, and then arranged the results onto a grid of 31 monitors, one for each day of the month. When taken as a whole, the effect tends to be painterly, with overall washes of blues, greens, and oranges.

In recent years, dozens of video artists, including Jean-Luc Godard, Sophie Calle, Julia Scher, Ann-Sofi Sidén, Kutluğ Ataman, and Deborah Stratman, have used surveillance to explore notions of the body, identity, portraiture, and the social value of both art and the media. But if surveillance in the traditional sense was about scopophilia (as in Warhol), it has become far less libidinous in these works. Lorna Simpson's *31* (2003) presents the viewer with 31 individual monitors, one for each day of the month. And over the course of 20 minutes, we watch an unknown woman get up, get ready for work, and go about her day on 31 different occasions. Yet the effect is not one of duration, as in Chantal Akerman's *Jeanne Dielman, 23 Quai du Commerce, 1080 Bruxelles*, but a formal collage, where the woman's life is presented all at once and becomes a colorful tapestry of movement and shape.

Portraiture has a close cousin in autobiography, which has its own rich cinematic history. Commercial filmmakers have often based their films on their personal experiences. But in the 1970s and 1980s, during the peak of the anti-aesthetic movement in the United States, a number of artists went further by using intimate mediums such as Super 8 and video to deliberately bring the moving image back into the realm of the body, the domestic, and the authentic. That is when Chick Strand, Daniel Eisenberg, Willie Varela, Su Friedrich, Nina Fonoroff, Susan

Mogul, and Shigeko Kubota began to explore autoethnography and confessional modes of address as an act of self-determination. Walter Benjamin's description of autobiography, which "has to do with time, sequence, and what makes the continuous flow of life," could act as a fitting description for Kubota's life-long project, where she has been documenting herself with a video camera since 1970.

And then there are those who explore similar ideas by adopting fictional characters to portray in their films and videos. In such cases, the work often explores how subjectivity is mediated through role models suggested by pop culture. The American video artist Eleanor Antin often makes artworks from the perspective of wholly invented personas, each with their own detailed backgrounds and personal possessions. What is more, she often places them into narrative films and videos

"You don't need to know where the beginning is, where the middle is, or where the end is … If I wanted to, I could create a film just about what we're doing here and now. But it would be a story perhaps on an emotional level."

Gregory Markopoulos

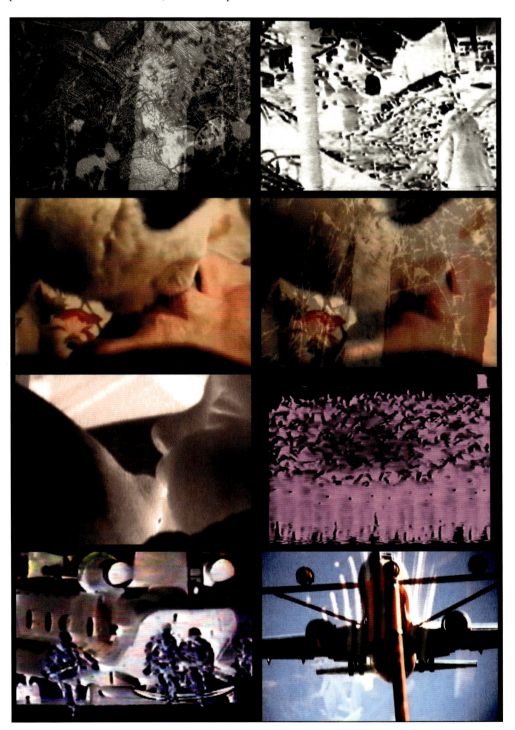

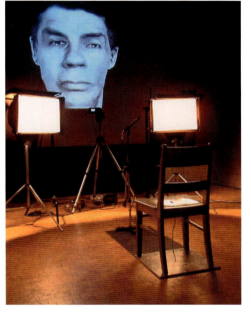

ABOVE
Installation view from 'Be Me' (2002)
Taking the autobiographical film to the extreme, Max Dean and Kristan Horton created an interactive work where each viewer's comments and facial expressions would be directly transposed onto a single image of Dean's face on a large screen.

LEFT
Stills from 'Devour' (2003–2004)
For this found-footage film, Carolee Schneemann used two screens to juxtapose scenes of innocence with mass violence.

ABOVE AND OPPOSITE
Stills from 'Ciao Bella' (2001)
One way for artists to explore social conventions
and stereotypes is to take on well-known
personas. In this work South African artist
Tracey Rose adopts 12 different characters
that are often attributed to people of color,
and gives each an individual scenario.

"When you respect the audience you don't
pitch to them. You do your very best and
give them the problem of coming to where
you've gone. The artist does his or her
utmost to create a path to that new place."

Ken Jacobs

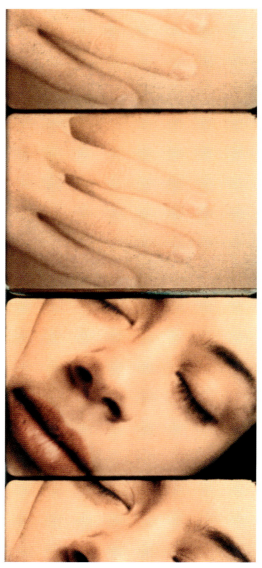

such as *The Last Night of Rasputin* (1989), an elaborately staged motion picture starring Eleanora Antinova (Antin) as the "famous" ballerina of the silent era. That in turn imbues her personal possessions, which she displays in gallery settings, with a palpable, albeit mythical, reality.

Bruce Conner, David Lamelas, Tracey Rose, Lynn Hershman Leeson, Mara Mattuschka, and Slater Bradley have all followed similar approaches. For them, surrogates allow them to reduce the world down to hackneyed scripts, masks, and screens, which in turn offers a particularly potent form of cultural criticism. The South African artist Tracey Rose made a multimedia piece, *Ciao Bella* (2001), where she appeared as 12 different characters all drawn from her own Catholic upbringing and her ancestry under apartheid. They included a gun-toting rebel, a sadomasochist, and an exotic diva named Hottentot Venus, who is paraded through London in the nude.

Max Dean and Kristan Horton, on the other hand, offer a more direct correspondence between the self and the screen in *Be Me* (2002), an installation piece that uses a digital camera and software programs to record the viewer's facial movements and voice in real time. That in turn manipulates a portrait of Dean's face in close-up, so that there is a literal, one-to-one relationship between the viewer and the projection.

Autobiography need not be so literal, however, especially in the intensely personal films of Stan Brakhage, Jonas Mekas, Jerome Hill, Andrew Noren, Carolee Schneemann, and Peter Hutton in the 1960s and 1970s. With these artists, autobiography becomes inseparable from the more abstract qualities of the lyrical genre, where there is a direct relationship between the formal properties of the image and the filmmaker's feelings, moods, and sensibilities.

"Music for light and mind" is how Andrew Noren has described his own autobiographical films of the period, and indeed the man who was the inspiration for Jim McBride's roman à clef, *David Holzman's Diary* (1967), has made a number of genuinely affecting celebrations of light and shadow. His 1968 effort, *Kodak Ghost Poems* (now called *Huge Pupils*) was, and still is, considered "the definitive 1960s self-portrait of the artist as a young boho," as J. Hoberman once described it; an utterly uncompromising reflection that includes what is often overlooked in most films—frank sexuality.

Since then, the New Mexico native has made nine autobiographical feature-length films under the heading of *The Adventures of the Exquisite Corpse*. Each reflects what Noren calls "backyard Buddha impersonations," where everyday domestic scenes are rendered directly, without judgment, and each exhibits his masterful grasp of timing, rhythm, and lyrical explosions of light. As Hoberman writes of 1987's *The Lighted Field*, "It's percussive in the extreme—light explodes off a cat's fur, a spring breeze has the velocity of a karate chop."

But it is New York's Jonas Mekas who is perhaps the best-known diarist in American avant-garde cinema. He began to craft his own impressionistic shooting style shortly after he took over the film reviews for *The Village Voice* in 1958, and it quickly evolved into a style as impressionistic as Noren's, although less aggressive or abstract. Indeed, with Mekas, the physical properties of the image—spontaneous frame bursts, solarizations, flares, accidents, and straight recordings—seem to convey his feelings, moods, and impressions with extraordinary precision. "When I am filming, I am also reflecting," writes Mekas. "I do not have much control over reality at all, and everything is determined by my memory, my past, so that this 'direct' filming becomes also a mode of reflection."

Such works have also spawned parodies and critiques. Germany's Lutz Mommartz made an irresistibly funny little film in 1967 called *Selbstschüsse*, which features Mommartz walking through an open field and literally playing with a camera to such a degree that it becomes a smitten lover. And the ever-inquisitive Hollis Frampton offered his own challenge to the autobiographical form with *(nostalgia)* (1971), a film that literally destroys a series of personal photographs one by one as the narrator describes the next photo the viewer is about to see. Here memory becomes the central motif, as the viewer continually tries to recall words that may or may not coincide with Frampton's burning photos.

Animation techniques can also be used to explore psychologically charged stories based on personal experiences. In recent years a number of talented filmmakers and contemporary artists have used both hand-drawn and cut-out figures to emphasize the psychological nature of the form. Lewis Klahr builds delirious, cut-out environs from vintage magazines, encyclopedias, medical texts, postcards, and advertisements to play out psychologically charged scenes that are inspired not only by his childhood, but also by his personal reaction to pop-cultural cues. His films, which include *The Pharaoh's Belt* (1993), *Altair* (1994), *Pony Glass* (1997), *Daylight Moon* (2002), and *Valise* (2004), recall the early pop art of Richard Hamilton, with their 1950s-style homes peopled with all-American comic-book characters. Yet Klahr, who is a master at the series form, refuses to ground his narratives in any particular genre. Rather, he builds feverish, elliptical tales that employ cross-cultural references—bouncing between film noir, melodrama, and pure abstraction in equal measure—to comment on mass consumerism, socially constructed identities, pleasure, and gender issues. "Like Jacques Tourneur," writes Mark McElhatten, "Klahr is a creator of atmospheres, not mere evocations of mood and setting, but ontological terrains where event and emotion register with archetypal power and dreamlike intensity."

ABOVE AND TOP
Stills from 'As I Was Moving Ahead Occasionally I Saw Brief Glimpses of Beauty' (2008)
Few filmmakers in the world have the ability to capture daily reality with the kind of lyricism that the New York–based Jonas Mekas has perfected over the years. Shot using a handheld Bolex, his diary films tend to be composed of quick frame bursts that reflect the rhythms and moods of each situation he is in. For this project he combined a number of his diary films (from 1970 to 1979) into what he later called a "love poem to New York."

RIGHT
Still from '10–16' (1997)
Beginning with audio recordings of average teenagers revealing their fears and frustrations, the British contemporary artist Gillian Wearing hired adult actors and asked them to lip-synch to the words. Here, Gary speaks with the voice of a 13-year-old boy who despises his lesbian mother.

Still from 'Altair' (1994)
While not a diarist, California-based Lewis Klahr often draws on personal remembrances or feelings to create exquisite, highly complex cut-out animation works. With this film, he uses his "interest in the 1940s," as he says, to create an elliptical tale culled from vintage women's magazines, which ultimately thrives on social and formal paradoxes.

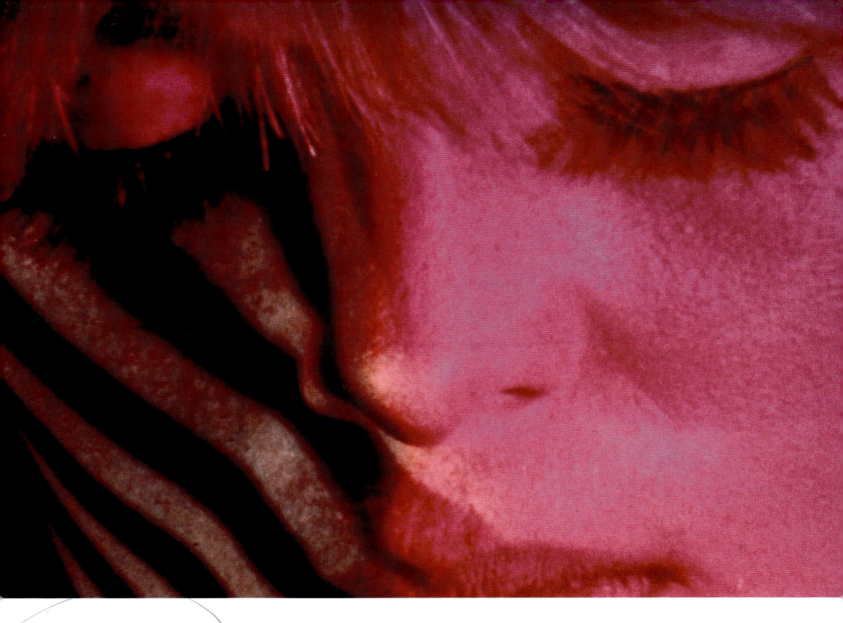

Still from 'Chelsea Girls' (1966)
Shot in 12 different rooms of New York's Chelsea Hotel (as a reference to Dante's 12 circles of Hell), and later displayed on two screens, in this film Andy Warhol's band of misanthropic hipsters carry on with typical narcissism: they vent, act out, preen, and pose.

watch! looks interesting!

Screen Tests (1964–1966)

Although they were often dismissed by critics at the time, Andy Warhol's *Screen Tests* have become a key reference point for an entire generation of younger contemporary artists working in both film and video.

Made between the years 1964 and 1966, they began casually enough, with Warhol shooting his friends doing the most mundane things. But they quickly became a bit more formal, where the sitter would take a seat on a stool and stare directly into the camera. (At the time they weren't called "screen tests" but "portraits" or "stillies"—a play on the word *movies*.)

More than 400 of these portraits are said to exist, although Warhol undoubtedly shot many more. And they offer a rare and privileged view of New York's elite in the mid-1960s, with subjects such as Bob Dylan, Lou Reed, Nico, Dennis Hopper, Sally Kirkland, Marcel Duchamp, Salvador Dalí, Ivy Nicholson, Susan Sontag, Edie Sedgwick, Jack Smith, Jonas Mekas, Jane Holzer, Paul America, Mary Woronov, and Francesco Scavullo.

Warhol generally manned the camera, although he occasionally had help from Gerard Malanga, Billy Linich, Paul Morrissey, and later Dan Williams. They also changed depending on Warhol's mood. Some were shot in close-up and some at medium length; some in black-and-white and some in color; and some grouped

ABOVE
**Stills from 'Nico' (1966) and 'Dennis Hopper'
(1964)**
As in most of Warhol's *Screen Tests*, each
subject is directed to sit motionless for a single
roll of 16mm film and just "be." Yet most
subjects, including those here, tend to become
self-aware and attempt to show only what they
want to show.

BELOW
Still from 'Bike Boy' (1967)
Andy Warhol's film follows the misadventures of
Joe Spencer, aka "Bikey," as he encounters a
series of oddball characters who seem bent on
attacking his masculinity. Here he meets Viva.

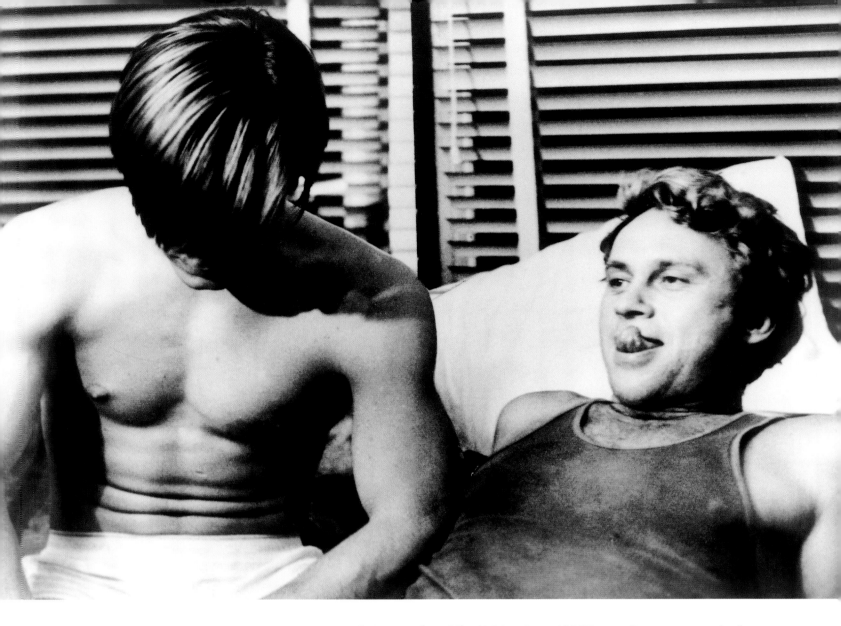

Still from 'Flesh' (1968)
Andy Warhol and director Paul Morrissey attempted to subvert the Hollywood melodrama with this film, which follows the exploits of a young junkie (Joe Dallesandro, left) who pulls tricks to pay for his wife's abortion and his drug habit.

into compilations such as *The 13 Most Beautiful Women*. Some were rarely shown at all. Similarly, the subjects themselves often contributed to the overall effect, whether they performed (Harry Smith), spun on their stools (James Rosenquist), or ate bananas (Philip Fagan).

Nonetheless, they all bore Warhol's unmistakable stamp, which, according to Stephen Koch, reveals his not-so-latent fetish for *looking*. "Even more than it does in most movies," he writes, "voyeurism dominates all Warhol's early films and defines their aesthetic ... [these films] reconstruct in their eventless essentials a kind of paradigm, a structured filmic model of the voyeur's relation to the world."

"The poet has not a 'personality' to express, but a particular medium in which impression and experience combine in particular and unexpected ways."

Maya Deren

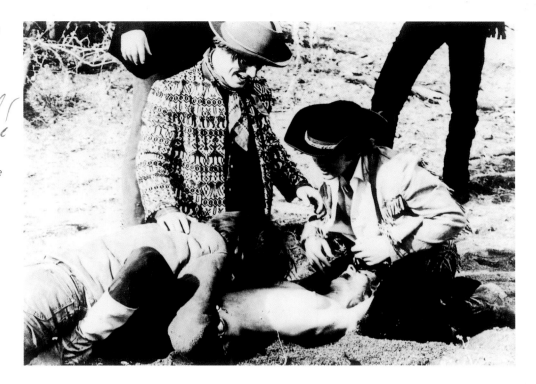

Still from 'Lonesome Cowboys' (1968)

For this decidedly iconoclastic, amateurish film, Warhol, as director, subverts the western genre by trading cowhands and gunslingers with drag queens and New York hipsters.

Still from 'My Hustler' (1965)

A crucial film in gay cinema history, Warhol's camp melodrama was categorized by *The Village Voice* as "a devastating scrutiny of socio-sexual mores."

Dada, Parody, Camp, and the Remake

The Dada film generally refers to a very short period of film history, and yet its influence has been extraordinarily profound. After all, Dada is the embodiment of iconoclasm and irreverence, and virtually every generation since has seen its own Dada spirit.

The movement officially started in Zurich in 1916, when Hugo Ball, Tristan Tzara, and Richard Huelsenbeck transposed their frustration and disgust over social conditions, bourgeois complacency, and the horrors of World War I into biting, satirical works that were also downright hilarious. Indeed, for the first time in history, artists were able to use virtually any material imaginable—the more banal and nonsensical the better—in an effort to confuse and confound both critics and the public. For them humor was an apt metaphor for art itself, since humor cannot be restricted by rules, or "even ideas," as the painter Francis Picabia once said. Rather it "requires a state of openness where anything can happen."

In its time Dada inspired a handful of unique, albeit disparate, efforts by artists/ filmmakers, including Picabia and René Clair (*Entr'acte*, 1924), Marcel Duchamp (*Anemic Cinema*, 1926), Man Ray (*Le Retour à la Raison*, 1923), and Hans Richter (*Vormittagsspuk*, 1928). Each used a different filmic approach, but it was Richter's sense of juxtaposition that gave his films a playful yet utterly subversive sensibility, one that was often interpreted by authority figures as a dangerous threat to the status quo. "The means of association can be sheer magic," said Richter. "It can alter things from their core and bestow upon them new values, give them content that they never had before. In association, one has elements of a picture-language medium of film poetry."

Being far removed from Europe, many of the experimental filmmakers working in Los Angeles in the 1920s and 1930s found their own Dada spirit as a way to express their own irreverence. Yet, for them, iconoclasm was often born out of their distance from Europe, which led them to experiment with both form and content without the weight of history. The émigrés Robert Florey and Slavko Vorkapich gained a small reputation for their *The Life and Death of 9413—A Hollywood Extra* (1928), a short film that tells the tragic tale of an actor's humiliation and eventual decline. While now seen as a classic example of West Coast expressionism, with artificial sets, painted backdrops, and an innovative use of miniatures, the film can also be seen as a parody of the French avant-garde. That was also true of Roger

ABOVE AND OPPOSITE
Stills from 'Day is Done' (2006)
Beginning with found high-school photographs of teenage goths, California contemporary artist Mike Kelley extrapolated a number of scenarios, environments, and sculptures of his own creation, which in turn became a large-scale installation. At the center of the work is a feature-length video that gives life to the photographs through invented monologues, musical numbers, and religious spectacles.

"Anything that explains itself or justifies itself is vulgar."
Jean Cocteau

ABOVE
Still from 'The Love of Zero' (1927)

ABOVE AND MIDDLE
Stills from 'The Life and Death of 9413—A Hollywood Extra' (1928)
An early example of Hollywood turning on itself, Robert Florey and Slavko Vorkapich's film portrays a hellish ride through the movie industry with an inventive use of miniatures and expressionistic sets.

Barlow/Harry Hay/Le Roy Robbins's *Even—As You and I* (1937), a film about amateur filmmakers who make the film-within-a-film *The Afternoon of a Rubberband*, which contains send-ups of *Un chien andalou, Entr'acte, VormittagsSpuk*, and Sergei Eisenstein, among others.

A more radical strategy could be found in the work of France's Jean-Isidore Isou and Maurice Lemaître, two artists at the center of the lettrist movement of the 1950s. They not only practiced their own cinematic deconstruction, where films were chopped up and spit back out, but performed public provocations and protoconceptual strategies that were designed to debunk cinematic conventions from the inside out.

That in turn signaled the dawn of the 1960s counterculture movement, which marshaled in a new era of pop-infused Dada iconoclasm. The Lithuanian-born George Maciunas, in particular, initiated the neo-Dada Fluxus movement that began with music performances but quickly expanded into the cinematic. And, thanks to Maciunas, who acted as producer and distributor, the Fluxus movement produced some 40-odd films that all shared a deep desire to parody and discredit what was then considered to be "serious" experimental filmmaking. Dick Higgins lampooned the autobiographical techniques of both Stan Brakhage and Bruce Baillie in a film he called *Invocation of Canyons and Boulders (for Stan Brakhage)* (1966), which contained nothing more than a single shot of a mustachioed mouth moving as though eating. Yoko Ono, on the other hand, made a number of Fluxus films, including a sly homage to Warhol's *Sleep* called *Fly* (1970), where an intoxicated housefly traverses the flesh of a sleeping female nude.

Other artists, such as Cheiko Shiomi, George Brecht, and Eric Andersen, followed suit with their own playfully absurdist renderings. Their legacy can be seen in the purely conceptual work of Ernst Schmidt Jr. (*Nothing*, 1971), Takahiko Iimura (*Dead Movie*, 1964), and Louise Lawler (*A Movie Will Be Shown without the Picture*, 1979), where the artwork attempts to break with formalism altogether and remove any discussion of materiality or innate properties from the artwork once and for all. (Each film showed everything but the film itself.) As a result, both Fluxus and conceptual art became extreme strategies, or endgames, which reduced cinema down to little more than its idea.

Yet in a capitalistic society, where issues of property remain central, there are few techniques that are quite as controversial as that of the "readymade." The Dada artist Marcel Duchamp set the idea in motion when he famously placed a urinal in a gallery in 1917 and claimed it as art. Since then dozens of filmmakers have employed similar strategies, although mostly for different reasons. The French situationists, in particular, routinely appropriated existing films as part of their rejection of the popular media, which they said promoted passivity and fostered a "crippling subservience." "We should live in a constant state of revolution, newness, and consumption," said the situationist Guy Debord.

Thus the "theft of aesthetic artifacts from the past," as Debord described "détournement," was not only an artistic practice, but a revolutionary act with specific social and political connotations. One could détour *The Birth of a Nation* (1915) in such a way that it would "highlight its artistic value while putting its offending racism in its proper place," Debord argued.

The French intellectual René Viénet was then inspired to détour a 1972 kung-fu movie, *Tang shou tai quan dao (Crush)*, and completely replace the dialogue track with Marxist commentary. The result is a humorous sociopolitical adventure film

Still from 'The Love of Zero' (1927)
Both Robert Florey and Slavko Vorkapich were veterans of Hollywood, Florey being a writer and Vorkapich a master at special effects and montage sequences. This film, which tells the story of an enthusiastic young man and his obsession with a young woman, is lesser known than their subsequent works, but it shows an assured hand.

"*When you think about the way one looks at the world; the way one combines remembrances, the voices going on inside your head, eye movements; then one realizes what a falsehood Hollywood editing is. It leads one down a road of narrative, but it cuts most human experience out.*"

Tony Oursler

called *La dialectique peut-elle casser des briques?* (*Can Dialectics Break Bricks?* 1973), where a ragtag group of martial artists/proletarians go head-to-head with imperial guards/bureaucrats. But instead of speaking plot-driven dialogue they argue about oppression, violence, Ferdinand de Saussure, Jacques Lacan, and Marx.

The more recent collage work of San Francisco's Craig Baldwin continues in a similar, subversive vein. "What I'm trying to do," explains Baldwin, who holds screenings in a storefront gallery in San Francisco, where random bulletins, training films, and propaganda films are played back-to-back, "is come up with a feeling of some kind of possibility of film language that exists both within the fiction and nonfiction world, where we can see that all real stories, I mean real historical facts, sort of have a little narrative to them. And also that there's a little bit of documentary truth in fantasy."

To that end Baldwin builds original, epic-length, often bombastic fictions out of hundreds, even thousands, of preexisting sources. His *Tribulation 99: Alien Anomalies Under America* (1991) tells the story of how aliens invaded the Earth centuries ago, and how that eventually led to actual events (the 99 steps) including the Roswell incident, JFK's assassination, and U.S. intervention in Latin America. Here "truthful" nonfiction material is reworked to reveal an alternative—often comical—reading of the same history. "This neotribal kind of scavenging through the crumbs on the table," says Baldwin of what he called narrative pointillism, "to bricolage something beautiful—a patchwork—made up with incredible diversity, variety, and changes of texture, that's authentic. That's not some *a priori*, top-down, overdetermined, overproduced thing. It's an authentic response from the margin."

Subversion, parody, and appropriation also come together in a related artistic strategy: the remake. As the name suggests, this is where a filmmaker remakes a well-known film to both mock and celebrate its aesthetic values. These range from the deliberately campy remakes of Warhol and Paul Morrissey (*Flesh for Frankenstein,* 1973; *Blood for Dracula,* 1974) to the faux TV commercials and

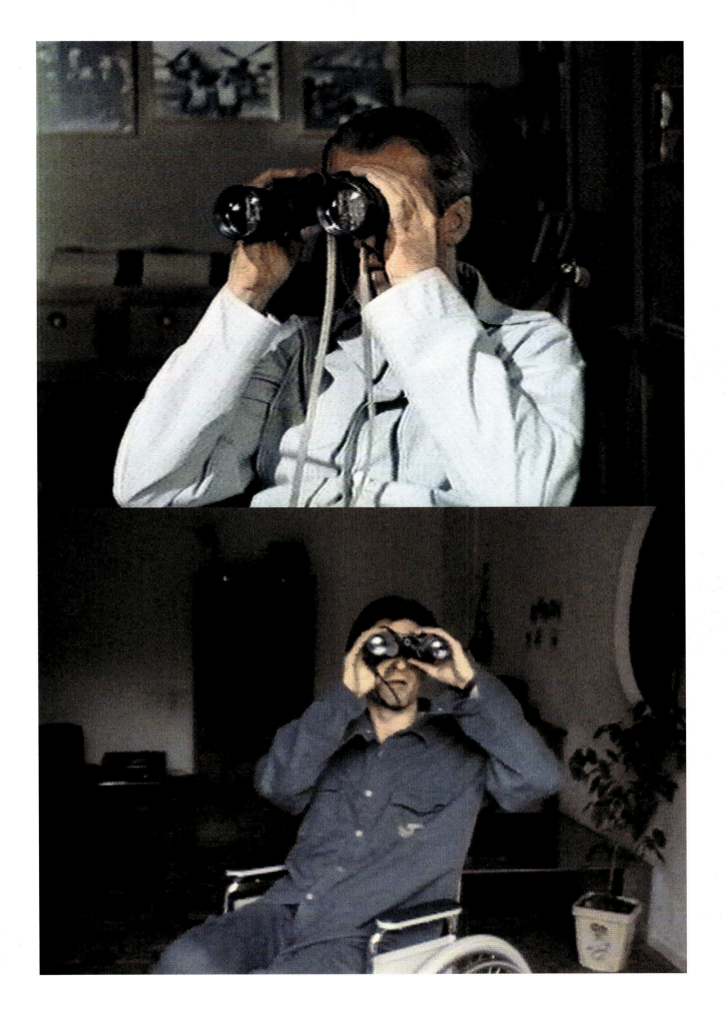

Stills from 'Love Film' (2004)
German contemporary artist Isabell Heimerdinger
hired professional actors and asked them to
perform a typical, Hollywood-style sex scene. It
ends with the pair discussing how "convincing"
they were, yet Heimerdinger makes no attempt to
let the viewer know whether that too was scripted
or improvised.

soap operas of Bruce and Norman Yonemoto. "The phenomenon of the remake,"
writes Jean-Christophe Royoux, "breaks with a conception of meaning in which
each stage implies that the preceding one is surpassed or disappears. In contrast
to this, the phenomenon of the remake implies the development of processes
of anamnesis, the dredging up of buried events and of 'things forgotten at the
beginning.'"

Like their peers working with found footage, the current generation of
installation artists—Douglas Gordon, James Coleman, Mark Lewis, Candice Breitz,
Joachim Koester, and Paul Pfeiffer—have begun to renegotiate the conventions of
the entertainment industry through large-scale environments defined by projected
images. For some, Hollywood represents the absolute apotheosis of the so-called
society of entertainment, which for many has contributed to the degradation of
personal expression. But for others, the process of cherry-picking scenes from
commercial films is an iconoclastic one, where Hollywood is revealed to be
a reflection of outdated, 19th-Century models. As the UK-based Mark Lewis
describes his own work in the late 1990s, "I would say that I'm looking for, and
identifying, precisely those inventions that happen despite, and more importantly
because of, the film's parasitical relationship to traditional forms: the novel and
theater."

Similarly, France's Pierre Huyghe repeatedly exploits the strange, curious place that exists between real life and reel life in his large-scale installation works. For *Remake* (1995) he hired a pair of nonactors and asked them to imitate scenes from Hitchcock's *Rear Window* (1954), which was itself an allegory for spectatorship. But Huyghe makes no attempt at fidelity or accuracy. Instead he instructs his two actors, who bear little, if any, resemblance to Grace Kelly and Jimmy Stewart, to read lines in the most natural (meaning awkward) manner imaginable. Thus the artist encourages viewers to think about established cinematic texts, or fictions, in the same way they think about actual historical events—as "remembered entities" with almost equal aesthetic values.

"Huyghe is concerned with the way in which a film is seen and experienced," writes Royoux, "how subtitles work, what kind of subjective baggage the viewer brings to the picture. He's convinced that as long as an experience is not individualized, the person involved remains subservient to all sorts of models and structures imposed on him."

That also holds true for the Swiss artist Christoph Draeger, who has laid bare not only the media's obsession with violence and catastrophe, but also its capacity to transform such horrific events into pure pleasure. His installation *Feel Lucky, Punk??!* (1997–2000) features a series of actors mouthing some of the more violent

ABOVE
Production still from 'Film' (1965)
Samuel Beckett's (left) only foray into filmmaking,
directed by Alan Schneider (second left), stands
as a key work in the history of metacinematic
works. It uses Bishop Berkeley's dictum, *"esse
est percipi"* or "to be is to be perceived," as a
jumping-off point, and features Buster Keaton
trying to avoid being seen by what he believes
is an all-seeing eye.

ABOVE RIGHT
Still from 'Pull My Daisy' (1959)
Robert Frank and Alfred Leslie's seminal film
began with a voice-over by Jack Kerouac,
working from one of his own plays. That was
then played back during production and lip-
synched to create a comic effect.

LEFT
Sequence from 'The Flower Thief' (1960)
With teddy bear in hand, underground star Taylor
Mead embodies the beat aesthetic by shunning
authority, breaking conventions, and mimicking
silent-film comedies. As a result, Ron Rice's first
film has been labeled an essential work in the
history of beat cinema.

OPPOSITE
Production still from 'The Crazy-Quilt' (1966)
Based on a short story by San Francisco's Dr.
Allen Wheelis, in this film director John Korty
(at camera) explores the relationship between
a man who expects nothing from life and a
woman who is an eternal optimist.

ABOVE
Still from 'Hallelujah the Hills' (1963)
A truly joyous farce by Adolfas Mekas, this film
follows the comic adventures of two overgrown
Boy Scouts who fall in love with the same girl.

OPPOSITE
**Still from 'Oiley Peloso the Pumph Man'
(1964–65)**
Made during his stint as the director of a mime
troop, Robert Nelson's film is one of his rarest
works. It uses a collage aesthetic to weave
together a series of seemingly random moments,
some comic, some sweet, including this
repeating motif of two nudes frolicking on a
swing.

TOP AND ABOVE
Production stills from 'Flaming Creatures' (1963)
Jack Smith's notorious film, one of the true
landmarks of the 1960s underground, was
initially inspired by Hollywood adventure films
of the 1940s, most notably those with actress
Maria Montez and *Ali Baba and the Forty
Thieves* (1944). Yet Smith's aesthetic was
rooted in a proto-pop-art style, which was more
impressionistic and gestural. Thus, in his hands,
a harem became an unlikely meeting ground for
a group of merry hipsters who end up in a wild,
surprisingly graphic, orgy.

RIGHT
Still from 'The Golden Positions' (1971)
James Broughton's best-known work from the
early 1970s uses average men and women,
from all walks of life, and entirely in the nude,
to recreate mundane social moments in static,
tableau form.

*"Art is not something to superimpose over
everyday life. If it's any good it always has to
come from everyday life."*

Jack Smith

lines from the likes of *Dirty Harry* (1971), *Magnum Force* (1973), *Taxi Driver* (1976),
and *Pulp Fiction* (1994) in bare, nondescript rooms. Unlike Huyghe, however,
Draeger places his scenes in a parallel construction with the actual footage from the
originals. We see a blond-haired man bearing little resemblance to Clint Eastwood
mimicking Dirty Harry, while the "real" Dirty Harry carries out his own acts
of cinematic violence on an adjacent screen. Thus Draeger forces the viewer to
recognize amateurism itself as being more "real" than its Hollywood counterpart,
and also that the original remains as absurd as, if not more absurd than, the parody.
"The use of medial aggregate states is insidious and confusing," writes Christoph
Doswald of Draeger's work, "because it raises endless questions about the function
and meaning of pictures in an endless process of deconstruction, decontextualization,
reconstruction, and recontextualization."

By contrast, Isabell Heimerdinger has attempted to tease out the various ways
in which Hollywood has infected our collective memories in her photo-based work
and installations. For her recent *Love Film* (2004) she hired two actors and directed
them to act out a Hollywood sex scene (a sly nod to both Vito Acconci and Susan
Mogul's sexually provocative works of the 1970s and 1980s). Since the actors have
never met, they awkwardly fumble their way through a semierotic nude love scene
for nearly two minutes until, finally, they seem to relax and discuss the experience.
"Do you think it looked real?" one asks. But as viewers, we have no way of knowing
if *any* aspect of the film is "real" or "acted," which is precisely Heimerdinger's point.
Where does fiction start? And does it ever end?

Nonetheless, in the arsenal of artistic techniques that a filmmaker can use,
amateurism remains one of the most controversial. The American beat poets and
filmmakers of the 1950s, in particular, developed their own anti-aesthetic as a way
to bring immediacy and honesty back into art. As the composer John Cage summed
up the prevailing ethos, "art should be the affirmation of life [and] not an attempt
to bring order out of chaos or suggest improvements in creation; but simply a way
of waking up to the very life we are living."

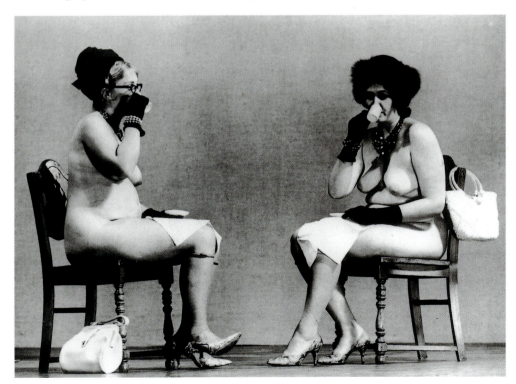

Still from 'Flaming Creatures' (1963)
Scenes such as this led to widespread rumors of pornography, which in turn led to constant raids by the New York Police Department and an obscenity case that wound up in the Supreme Court. As a result, Smith's film is the only experimental work to be described in the Congressional Record in graphic detail.

Thus chance, spontaneity, and rawness became the hallmarks of artistic expression for the beats. As a result, filmmakers responded by emphasizing the temporal aspects of their films, often through diary techniques or a loose, improvisatory style, where the film becomes a record of the filmmaker's "performance."

Ron Rice, whose personal extravagance was matched only by his influence as a filmmaker, made one of the most influential experimental films of the early 1960s, *The Flower Thief* (1960). This rollicking, ultra-low-budget affair, which he made with Vernon Zimmerman, featured a Chaplinesque tramp (Taylor Mead) wandering through a series of alternatively silly and wistful pranks. While anachronistic, the film's attitude became an emblem for the beats. As critic Jonas Mekas points out, its happy-go-lucky character captured the new generation's longing for independence and frustration with social constraints. "The idiot today is the only character through which a poet can reveal the beauty of living," wrote Mekas. "Salinger chose children. The entire beat generation chose idiocy. The idiot [and the beat] is above [or under] our daily business, money, morality … That is why *The Flower Thief* is one of the most original creations of the recent cinema."

Rice was not alone, however. Similar themes could be found in the freewheeling films of Sidney Peterson (*The Lead Shoes*, 1949), James Broughton (*Loony Tom, the Happy Lover*, 1951), Robert Frank and Alfred Leslie (*Pull My Daisy*, 1959), Ken Jacobs (*Blonde Cobra*, 1963), Robert Nelson (*King Ubu*, 1963), and John Korty (*The Crazy-Quilt*, 1966).

Yet few filmmakers were quite as influential as Jack Smith. Born in 1932 in Columbus, Ohio, Smith moved to New York in the late 1950s, and quickly earned a reputation for absolute unpredictability and irreverence. His first love was experimental theater, which he quickly overturned and disrupted with his own, utterly unique, sensibility. But it was his film work that brought him international attention. As Andy Warhol would say later, "he was the only person I would ever try to copy."

At the heart of Smith's aesthetic was a deliberate amateurism that was defined by a loose, improvisatory camera, extravagant/eroticized mise-en-scène, and a tongue-in-cheek, utterly faux rendering of Hollywood and its star system. His notorious short *Flaming Creatures* (1963) was designed to mock the overheated, exotic adventure movies of Hollywood's Golden Age. Yet instead of a story, he reduced the plot down to a few gestures and a single set: a faux harem where his "stars"—beatniks, transvestites, and Spanish dancers—pair off and engage in a playful, but surprisingly graphic, orgy.

That film, which ignited a firestorm of controversy over its sexual frankness, pushed the art film into the realm of pure camp. As Susan Sontag wrote in 1964 in her influential essay "Notes on 'Camp'," the word itself comes from the French verb *camper*, meaning to perform or strike a pose. Thus, "campiness" connotes pretending, or any work of art that is rich with exaggeration and self-awareness. That serves as a fitting description for much of the so-called underground films of the 1960s, including the over-the-top parodies of Rudy Burckhardt and Red Grooms (*Shoot the Moon*, 1962; *Lurk*, 1964–1965) and the grotesquely humorous films of Robert Nelson and William T. Wiley (*The Great Blondino*, 1967).

ABOVE
Still from 'Shoot the Moon' (1962)
Rudy Burckhardt and painter Red Grooms collaborated on a number of pop-art farces in the 1960s, most notably this one, which toys with the Georges Méliès' film of the same name.

TOP
Still from 'The Secret of Wendel Samson' (1966)
Using wildly expressive sets and costumes, Mike Kuchar's film follows Wendel (Red Grooms) as he struggles with breaking up with his boyfriend. But when a female friend pressures him into a relationship, it sends him into a nightmarish world full of violent imagery and over-the-top punishments.

RIGHT
Still from 'Sins of the Fleshapoids' (1965)
Mike Kuchar's epic Super 8 film was devised as a homespun sci-fi extravaganza, complete with mad robots running amok and taking refuge in a young woman's home.

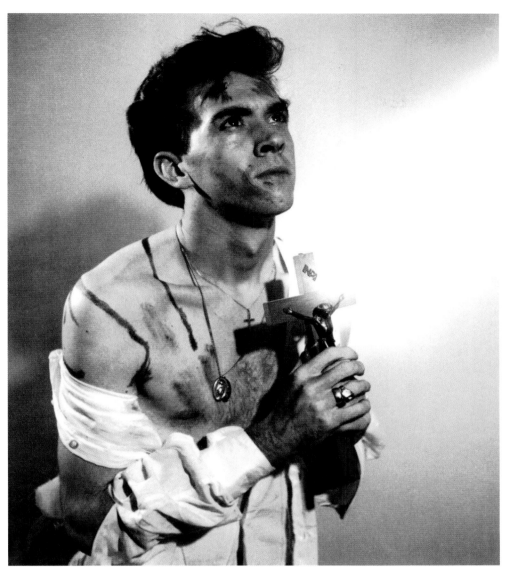

ABOVE
Still from 'Hallelujah the Hills' (1963)

TOP LEFT
Still from George Kuchar 8mm film
In the 1950s, George Kuchar and his twin brother, Mike, began producing ultra-low-budget underground versions of Hollywood genre films, with names like *I Was a Teenage Rumpot* and *The Devil's Cleavage*. These 8mm kitchen-sink masterpieces positioned the Kuchar brothers as the Bronx's answer to the downtown underground filmmaking scene, which quickly adopted the Kuchars as their own. Now working on video, George Kuchar has made over 200 films.

Such films embraced an anti-aesthetic of deliberate artificiality and faux Hollywood drama, which in turn inspired an entire generation of younger filmmakers of the 1970s. For them, larger gauges such as 16mm and 35mm were too professional and beyond their means, so many, including George and Mike Kuchar, Saul Levine, Willie Varela, Mañuel DeLanda, and Stan Brakhage, embraced smaller gauges to further enhance the handmade quality of their work. "Eight millimeter and Super 8 was a movement that produced a huge body of work," explains Steve Anker. "And it is my opinion that the content of such works is very much informed by the medium; so much so, that I would argue that it's an aesthetic in itself."

That was also true for an entire generation of UK filmmakers, including Derek Jarman, Cerith Wyn Evans, and Sophie Muller, who were associated with the so-called British New Romantic movement of the late 1970s and early 1980s. That movement earned its name for its deliberate return to a more visceral, emotionally charged cinema, one that deliberately turned its back on the "stale" formalism of the structuralist film and embraced instead a romantic idealism.

Meanwhile, New York and San Francisco saw the emergence of the so-called Cinema of Transgression, which married the rawness of performance art with a more violent, ironical, often sadistic bent culled from punk rock. Indeed, if Dada was "an indefinable intoxication," as Hugo Ball once described it, and a complete

"I really don't believe in the difference between documentary and fiction. Take for example a film with Marilyn Monroe. If you look at it 20 years later it has become a documentary on Marilyn Monroe, and of course a document of an era. The same goes for the material in which the film was made."

Chantal Akerman

Still from 'Lütte mit Rucola' (2006)
German contemporary artist John Bock has developed his unique aesthetic through the lens of Dada, bricolage, and "failurist" sensibilities. In the process he creates expressive, theatrical performances and videos that transform common materials, constructions, and props into pieces of sculpture. For this project, Bock has taken on the role of a sadistic scientist who goes back and forth between mutilating a man in his lab and having a heart-to-heart with his daughter in the other room. For Bock, the performance touches on cinematic violence, religion, and sacrifice.

and total dedication to collision, chaos, and sensory overload, the punk generation brought that squarely into the postmodern age. Here Georges Bataille's description of "hate as being the only emotion that can advance to real poetry" finds its cinematic equivalent. Richard Kern's *Fingered* (1986) paints a disturbing portrait of New York street life, where the body is routinely attacked, violated, and put on display. This is a world of unrepentant rage, immediate gratification, and raw (and unsimulated) sex.

This is also when narrative returned to the art film, both as a way to reintroduce storytelling and as a way to luxuriate in the sheer visceral, decorative quality of baroque excess. Indeed, like their predecessors in the mid-1960s—Anger with his demonology, Koji Wakamatsu with his extreme violence, and Vilgot Sjöman with his overt sexual frankness—the filmmakers of the 1980s and early 1990s imbued their films with the collective frustration, rage, and guilt of their generation. They include artists and filmmakers such as Peggy Ahwesh, Beth B., Nick Zedd, Luther Price, Tessa Hughes-Freeland, Laura Parnes, Ian Kerkhof, Joe Gibbons, Tony Oursler, the Duvet Brothers, Ursula Pürrer, Mara Mattuschka, Angela Hans Scheirl, and even such experimental commercial film directors as David Cronenberg.

Parody and subversion took a slightly different turn in Europe, however, where pop art was less an affront than it was an essential bulwark against the devastation of war and class distinctions. It was this environment that spawned the sardonic

films of Rainer Werner Fassbinder, who often filled his films with clichés culled from American TV and cinema. For filmmaker-critic Stephen Dwoskin, that is a constructive, rather than a negative, criticism. "In *Warnung vor einer heiligen Nutte* [*Beware of a Holy Whore*, 1971]," he writes, "even the camera angles, tracking shots, and the traditional language of film are blown up to seem like clichés, [which is to say] he takes the conventions of mainstream cinema—flamboyant characters, extreme behavior, expressive camerawork—and renders them empty, as mere signs representing little more than themselves."

West Germany's Werner Nekes, on the other hand, made a number of beautifully impressionistic, subversive films that use parody and misanthropy with equal measure. In 1968 he transformed an 8mm film of *Tarzan* into a sardonic collage called *Tarzan's Kampf mit dem Gorilla* (1968) that emphasizes bestiality to great comedic effect. Similarly, the always-sardonic Werner Schroeter made *Neurasia* (1968), a dramatized rehearsal for a soap opera where every aspect—from flat lighting to cardboard acting—could be read as a cliché of a cliché. By contrast Austria's Peter Tscherkassky exposed the very foundation of the social fabric in *Happy-End* (1996), a hilarious found-footage film that deftly reworks some home movies of a vivacious elderly couple in Vienna, where we see them over a series of Christmas celebrations.

ABOVE, LEFT AND RIGHT
Stills from 'Gummo' (1997)
Eschewing linear plot devices and adopting a neorealist style, Harmony Korine's debut as a director weaves together seemingly unrelated events in a common suburban housing tract to paint a disturbing portrait of Americana.

BELOW LEFT
Still from 'Killing Friends' (2002)
Stripping away camp elements from typical exploitation films, the California-based artist Julian Hoeber attempts to marry the kind of static camerawork found in the work of minimalists like Bruce Nauman, and the outright gore found in cheap horror films.

LEFT
Still from 'The Gore Trilogy' (2006)
Italian contemporary artist Francesco Vezzoli has long been interested in mining celebrity culture—especially actual celebrities—in his performance pieces and videos. For this film he created a mock "coming attraction" for a celebrity-filled, indulgent, Hollywood-style spectacle that picks up where Gore Vidal's *Caligula* (1979) left off.

BELOW
Stills from 'A Family Finds Entertainment' (2004)
Using wildly painted sets, costumes, and colored makeup, Rhode Island's Ryan Trecartin channels the ghost of Jack Smith by telling a hyperkinetic, comic tale of a group of teens who exist in a psychedelic world of their own. There's Skippy, the suicidal boy trying to come out of the closet; Shin, who leads a band of hipsters into a life of "randomness"; and, of course, the family dog.

"[Let's have] a cinema of artistic expression, or more particularly, an instrument of poetry, with all this word possesses of a liberating sense; of a subversion of reality; of a threshold of the marvelous world of the subconscious; of a nonconformity with the mean-spirited world surrounding us."

Luis Buñuel

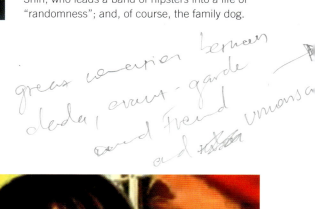

And, more recently, there has been a return to some of the more visceral, expressive qualities of 1960s underground cinema, with echoes of Jack Smith's overt immediacy. They include the deliberate amateurism of Mike Kelley, Cameron Jamie, Marcel Dzama, Ryan Trecartin, Sadie Benning, Sue de Beer, and Janice Findley; the *Jackass*-inspired provocations of Harmony Korine, Nao Bustamante, and Jesse Sugerman; and the more conceptual comedy of Martin Kersels, Francesco Vezzoli, John Bock, Christian Jankowski, Andrew Kötting, Miguel Calderón, Nguyen Tan Hoang, and Hélio Oiticica.

"My art is about the everyman," explains Kersels, who often evokes Samuel Beckett and Ernie Kovacs in his humorous films and installations. "And sometimes the everyman can be pretty funny."

On the Marriage Broker Joke as Cited by Sigmund Freud in Wit and Its Relation to the Unconscious, or Can the Avant-Garde Artist Be Wholed? (1977–1979)

Owen Land's *On the Marriage Broker Joke as Cited by Sigmund Freud in* Wit *and Its Relation to the Unconscious, or Can the Avant-Garde Artist be Wholed?* (1977–1979) uses the Dada and futurist method of appropriation and destabilized meaning to create one of the true masterpieces of avant-garde cinema.

Made and remade in the late 1970s, the film begins with a close-up of a woman experiencing an orgasm and quickly evolves into a series of palindromes and puns. The theological text from Evelyn Underhill's *Mysticism* (1911) crawls over the sex scene while describing a religious experience and the nature of ecstasy. A short time later, we are introduced to a nerdy filmmaker (Morgan Fisher), who recites an "ode to the sprocket hole," which in turn leads to a textual error dealing with the word *pander*, as detailed by Freud's discussion of sexual meaning in marriage-broker jokes. (As Land points out, the only jokes included in Freud's examination of humor are Jewish jokes about marriage brokers and panders. "Freud didn't have any good material," explains Land. "He would have bombed in Vegas.")

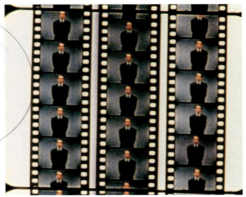

Thus *pander* becomes *pandas*, and Land includes a scene of two actors in panda costumes who are seen relaxing in a modernist home. After a discussion about the avant-garde, they make an experimental film inspired by Marriage Broker Plums, an actual brand of Japanese salted plums. Thus, as the triple pun in the title suggests, the entire film continually takes off on tangents, yet always returns to an ever-so-sly attack on the avant-garde's obsession with using film to create holistic, subjective experiences of ecstatic (and sexual) reverie.

But that wasn't Land's only attempt at parody. His famous *Wide Angle Saxon* (1975) is filled with similar word games and misadventures, including an episode with a character, Earl Greaves, who experiences an epiphany after being bored to tears watching an experimental film at the Walker Art Center (made by Al Rutcurts, an anagram of "structural"). That in turn convinces him to rid himself of his material possessions in the manner of Saint Augustine, which in turn leads to more cinematic puns.

Indeed, with these films, parody achieves a level of sophistication that remains unparalleled in both experimental and mainstream circles. As P. Adams Sitney says, Land, who also made films under the name George Landow, "has produced a coherent body of aggressively original films and has asserted, through those films, a unique position in opposition to the very genre in which he works."

Stills from 'On the Marriage Broker Joke as Cited by Sigmund Freud in *Wit* and Its Relation to the Unconscious, or Can the Avant-Garde Artist be Wholed?' (1977–79)
Owen Land, who often goes by the name George Landow, is one of few artists able to bring a genuine Duchampian humor to the cinema. For this film he plays off the jokes included in Freud's classic study of sex and humor, but transposes "panderers" with a pair of "pandas" who attempt to make an experimental film.

Chronology

1919–1921 Robert Wiene's *Das Kabinett des Doktor Caligari* (*The Cabinet of Dr. Caligari*, 1919), Germaine Dulac's *La Fête espagnole* (1920), and other feature-length experiments begin to exploit avant-garde ideas and signal a convergence of commercial and avant-garde practices. Meanwhile, Charles Sheeler and Paul Strand create the first city symphony and Walter Ruttmann begins to define the absolute film with experiments in cinematic abstraction.

1922–1924 André Breton's manifesto of surrealism announces a new avant-garde preoccupation with the subconscious, while Oskar Fischinger begins his wax-animation experiments en route to his discovery of visual music. Dada gets its first genuine Dada film, *Entr'acte* (1924), by René Clair and Francis Picabia.

1925–1927 The Russian avant-garde develops its own theories of montage in the service of

revolution, with Lev Kuleshov releasing his theory of the three-shot model and Sergei M. Eisenstein publishing his theories of a "materialist" approach to film. "We do not need kino-glaz, but kino-fist!" writes Eisenstein. "Soviet film must smash skulls!"

1928–1931 Luis Buñuel and Salvador Dalí release *Un chien andalou* (1929); the German authorities deem Hans Richter a Bolshevik threat after seeing his film, *Alles dreht sich, alles bewegt sich* (1929); Jean Cocteau's *Le sang d'un poète* (*The Blood of a*

Poet, 1930) is deemed a "parasite on the body of surrealism" by the surrealists; and a group of right-wing radicals bursts into a screening of Buñuel and Dalí's *L'Âge d'Or* (1930) and a small-scale riot ensues.

1932–1937 The European avant-garde movement dissipates in the wake of both political turmoil and the introduction of sound film. New factions of experimentation emerge in the UK and the United States. Len Lye makes an early "camera-less" film, *A Color Box* (1935); Joseph Cornell creates an early found-footage film, *Rose Hobart* (1936); and Oskar Fischinger experiments with three-color process on *Kreise* (*Circles*, 1933).

1938–1947 A more rigorous experimentation with form can be seen in both mainstream and avant-garde film: Orson Welles's *Citizen Kane* (1941) uses extreme depth of field and overlapping dialogue, Italy's Mario Serandrei calls for a "neorealism," and Maya Deren and Alexander Hammid release *Meshes of the Afternoon* (1943).

1948–1953 The end of World War II ushers in a new era for experimental film in America. The beat movement embraces a return to Dada, and "underground" artists find inspiration in abstract expressionism and action painting. Akira Kurosawa offers new challenges to narrative with *Rashômon* (1950), and Maya Deren presents her theory on dual-axis poetics.

1954–1957 A period of great creative experimentation. Filmmakers see themselves in

ABOVE
Production still from 'Shadows' (1959)
John Cassavetes's breakthrough underground film, which follows three siblings as they try to make it in New York City, was instrumental in jump-starting the independent-film movement of the 1960s.

RIGHT
Production still from 'The Blood of a Poet'
('Le sang d'un poète', 1930)

direct opposition to the mainstream. Robert Breer develops his single-frame collage films, Kenneth Anger releases his Aleister Crowley–inspired *Inauguration of the Pleasure Dome* (1954–1966), Peter Kubelka develops his "metric film" theory, and Harry Smith starts his *Mirror Animations* (1956–1957).

1958–1962 The art film continues to strive for greater purity, which divides filmmakers in both Europe and the United States. On the one hand, Alfred Lesley and Robert Frank's *Pull My Daisy* (1959) and John Cassavetes's *Shadows* (1959) usher in a new, improvisatory style of filmmaking, which is mirrored by Jean-Luc Godard's *À bout de souffle* (*Breathless*, 1960). On the other hand, Stan Brakhage moves cinema away from its third-person address with *Anticipation of the Night* (1958), and Alain Resnais (*Hiroshima mon amour*, 1959), Michelangelo Antonioni (*L'avventura*, 1960), and Chris Marker (*Lettre de Sibérie*, 1957) push cinema into deeper, subjective realms.

1963–1966 Pop art flourishes and ignites a new era of conceptual (and cynical) strategies. Andy Warhol makes *Sleep* (1963), and Susan Sontag publishes "Notes on 'Camp'" (1964). Underground film hits critical mass, with Jack Smith's *Flaming Creatures* (1963) landing in court on obscenity charges, and George Maciunas, Nam Jun Paik, and Owen Land forging new minimalist paths.

1967–1968 A highly productive period of experimentation, with a newly established canon of films and filmmakers, and extensive media coverage. The image falls siege to intense philosophical and ideological debates. Guy Debord publishes *La société du spectacle* (*The Society of the Spectacle*, 1967), Michael Snow completes *Wavelength* (1967), Czech cinema revives surrealism, and both Jordan Belson and Stanley Kubrick attempt to push cinema into the realm of pure mind expansion.

1969–1971 The art film strives for greater legitimacy. Structuralism peaks with Godard making *British Sounds* (1969), Hollis Frampton making *Zorns Lemma* (1970), and Ken Jacobs détourning *Tom, Tom, the Piper's Son* (1969). International filmmakers begin to incorporate heavy doses of allegory, surrealism, and collage techniques, leading to Alejandro Jodorowsky's *El Topo* (1970) and Dušan Makavejev's *W.R.: Misterije organizma* (*W.R.: Mysteries of the Organism*, 1971).

1972–1975 Feminist theory, minority cinemas, and the dissolution of both journals and funding for experimental works result in a crisis for the avant-garde, which leads to a radical balkanization of the art film and the emergence of ironic parodies, including René Viénet's *La dialectique peut-elle*

casser des briques? (*Can Dialectics Break Bricks?* 1973) and the Kuchar Brothers' Super 8 camp affairs. The installation film gains increasing momentum with Michael Snow's *Two Sides to Every Story* (1974), and performance artists such as Paul McCarthy renegotiate the shock value of Actionism.

1977–1986 The postmodern sensibility and a radical swing to the right inspires a new era of challenging, self-reflexive bricolage with Derek Jarman's *Jubilee* (1977), David Cronenberg's *Videodrome* (1983), and Raúl Ruiz's *L'Hypothèse du tableau volé* (*The Hypothesis of the Stolen Painting*, 1979). Video art becomes a legitimate medium, and David Lynch releases his neosurrealist *Eraserhead* (1977).

1987–1995 Experimental and mainstream filmmakers return to more sensuous, deliberately beautiful, forms ranging from Wong Kar-wai's *A Fei jing juen* (*Days of Being Wild*, 1991) to Pat O'Neill's *Water and Power* (1989). A new wave of conceptualism inspires installation artists to deal with ideas of appropriation, duration, and installation work without sacrificing the lushness of the image. The emergence of digital technologies fosters Douglas Gordon's *24 Hour Psycho* (1993), Bill Viola's *The Greeting* (1995), and Eija-Liisa Ahtila's *If 6 Was 9* (1995).

1996–present The emergence of video directors infiltrating Hollywood helps to ignite a new era of commercial/avant-garde film, with Spike Jonze's *Being John Malkovich* (1999), Christopher Nolan's *Memento* (2000), and Michel Gondry's *Eternal Sunshine of the Spotless Mind* (2004). Contemporary artists both deny and embrace cinema proper, with Pierre Huyghe's *L'Ellipse* (1998), Tacita Dean's *Fernsehturm* (2001), and Paul Sietsema's *Empire* (2002). Themes of interactivity, computational cinema, and multiplatform approaches begin to grow exponentially, suggesting a new dawn of film experimentation.

ABOVE
Production still from 'Me and My Brother' (1969)
Robert Frank directs a love scene.

LEFT
Production still from 'The Cool World' (1963)
Shirley Clarke directs a scene in her neorealist look at race relations in postwar America.

Filmography

Caribbean Pirates: Houseboat Party (2001–2005)
Crew: *Director-Camera-Actor* Paul McCarthy in collaboration with Damon McCarthy, *Videography* Naotaka Hiro, Damon McCarthy, Paul McCarthy, Anne Etheridge, *Video Production* Tatiana Bliss, *Associate Producer* Peter Kirby, *Technical Coordinator* Harry Dawson, *Asst. Camera Technicians* Brian Garbellini, David Thomas, *Grip Operators* Tim Herrman, Kim Bridwell, *Sound* J. E. Jack, *Video Editing* Damon McCarthy, Naotaka Hiro. 2005, 4-channel video, 3-screen projection, 1:32 minutes. Courtesy of the artist, Hauser & Wirth, Zürich, London.
Cast: Suzan Averitt (Martha), Melinda Ring (Village Boy), Ryan Templeton (Honey), Thomas Trafelet (George), Will Watkins (Villager, Nick).

Caribbean Pirates: Pirate Party (2001–2005)
Crew: *Director-Camera-Actor* Paul McCarthy in collaboration with Damon McCarthy, *Videography* Naotaka Hiro, Damon McCarthy, Paul McCarthy, Anne Etheridge, *Video Production* Tatiana Bliss, *Associate Producer* Peter Kirby, *Technical Coordinator* Harry Dawson, *Asst. Camera Technicians* Brian Garbellini, David Thomas, *Grip Operator* Tim Herrman, *Sound* J. E. Jack, *Video Editing* Damon McCarthy, Naotaka Hiro. 2005, 4/6-channel video, 4-screen projection, approximately 100 minutes. Courtesy of the artist, Hauser & Wirth, Zürich, London.
Cast: Cindy Clark, Emmy Collins, Jennifer Collins, Felicia Dannay, Christa De'Erynn, Jessica Hanna, Gary Kelley, Paul McCarthy, Craig McIntyre, Koby Moss, Jaime Richter, Melinda Ring, Ken Roht, David Shearer, Thomas Trafelot, Will Watkins, Holly Wellin, Stanislas Yombo.

Epilogue (2005)
Crew: *Director-Editor-Producer* Jordan Belson, *Producer* Cindy Keefer and the Center for Visual Music with support from the NASA Art program, commissioned by the Hirshorn Museum, *Music Isle of the Dead, Opus 29*, Sergei Rachmaninoff. 2005, video/film, 12 minutes.

The Decay of Fiction (2002)
Crew: *Director-Screenwriter-Editor-Producer* Pat O'Neill, *Producers* Rebecca Hartzell, Nancy Oppenheim, *Cinematographer-Sound Design* George Lockwood, *Sound* Cole Russing, *Wardrobe* Violetta Elfimova, *Supporters* The Rockefeller Foundation, The Guggenheim Memorial Foundation, Elizabeth Daley, Stephen F. Lawler, Marsha Kinder. Released 2002 by Lookout Mountain Films, 35mm, 73 minutes.
Cast: Wendy Windburn (Barbara), William Lewis (Bill), Julio Leopold (Johnnie), Amber Lopez (Helene), Jack Conley (Jack), John Rawling (George), Patricia Thielemann (Louise).

The Holy Mountain (1973)
Crew: *Director-Screenwriter* Alejandro Jodorowsky, *Producers* Alejandro Jodorowsky, Allen Klein, Robert Taicher, Roberto Viskin, *Director of Photography* Rafael Corkidi, *Art Directors* David Antón, José Durán, *Costumes* Micky Nichols, *Music* Don Cherry, Ronald Frangipane, Alejandro Jodorowsky, *Editors* Alejandro Jodorowsky, Federico Landeros, *Distributor* ABKCO. 1973, also released as *The Sacred Mountain* and *La Montaña sagrada*, color, 114 minutes.
Cast: Alejandro Jodorowsky (The Alchemist), Horácio Salinas (The Thief), Zamira Saunders (The Written Woman), Juan Ferrara (Fon), Adriana Page (Isla), Burt Kleiner (Klen), Valerie Jodorowsky (Sel), Nicky Nichols (Berg), Richard Rutowski (Axon), Luis Loveli (Lut), and Ana De Sade, Leticia Robles, Connie de La Mora, Pablo Leder, Re Debris, Guadalupe Perullers, Héctor Ortega, Robert Taicher, Manuel Dondé, Ramiro Chávez Gochicoa, and Jane Mitchell.

Mouchette (1967)
Crew: *Director* Robert Bresson, *Producer* Anatole Dauman, *Screenplay* Robert Bresson, Georges Bernanos, *Novel Nouvelle histoire de Mouchette*, Georges Bernanos, *Director of Photography* Ghislain Cloquet, *Production Design* Pierre Guffroy, *Art Director* Jean Catala, *Costumes* Odette Le Barbenchon, *Music* Jean Wiener, Claudio Monteverdi, *Editor* Raymond Lamy, *Distributor* Argos Films. October 26, 1967, black & white, 78 minutes.
Cast: Nadine Nortier (Mouchette), Jean-Claude Guilbert (Arsène), Maria Cardinal (Mother), Paul Hébert (Father), Jean Vimenet (Mathieu), Marie Susini (Mathieu's wife), Marine Trichet (Luisa), Raymonde Chabrun (Grocer).

On the Marriage Broker Joke as Cited by Sigmund Freud in *Wit* and Its Relation to the Unconscious, or Can the Avant-Garde Artist be Wholed? (1977–1979)
Crew: *Director-Editor-Producer* Owen Land, *Music* Johannes Ockeghem, *Distributor* LUX. Color, 16mm, 18 minutes.
Cast: Morgan Fisher, Paul Sharits, Bonita Lei, Yoshi, Owen Land.

Der Sandmann (1995)
Crew: *Director-Editor-Writer* Stan Douglas, *Producers* DAAD Berliner Kunstlerprogramm, The Whitney Biennial Exhibition (1995), *Cinematography* Martin Kukula, *Art Director* Susanne Hopf, *Costumes* Tatjana Krauskopf, *Editors* Stan Douglas, Birgit Berndt, *Sound Engineer* Martin Steyer, *Motion Control Software* Stock Final, *Projector Synchronization* Jean Darbesson. Premiered at the Whitney Biennial 1995 and DAAD Berliner, mixed media, looped.
Cast: Frank Odjidja (Natanael), Thomas Marquard (Lothar), Adelheit Kleineidam (Klara), Rudolf W. Marnitz (Coppelius/Sandmann).

Schwechater (1958)
Crew: *Director-Editor-Producer* Peter Kubelka, *Distributor* New York's Film Maker's Cooperative. Black and white, 16mm, 1:30 minutes.

Screen Tests (1964–1966)
Crew: *Director-Cameraman* Andy Warhol, *Assistants* Gerard Malanga, Billy Linich, Paul Morrissey, Dan Williams, *Distributor* Museum of Modern Art/The Warhol Foundation. More than 400 individual short films, black and white, silent, 16mm, approximately 4 minutes each.
Cast: (Abbreviated list) Edie Sedgwick, Nico, Jane Holzer, Ondine, Mario Montez, Mary Woronov, Ronnie Cutrone, Freddie Herko, Billy Linich, Ingrid Superstar, Ultra Violet, John Giorno, Paul America, Gerard Malanga, Sally Kirkland, Brooke Hayward, Beverly Grant, Ivy Nicholson, Ann Buchanan, Susan Bottomly, Dennis Hopper, John Cale, Donovan, Bob Dylan, Salvador Dalí, Marcel Duchamp, Jim Rosenquist, Niki de Saint Phalle, Allen Ginsberg, Ed Sanders, Edwin Denby, Jack Smith, Harry Smith, Marie Menken, Willard Maas, Taylor Mead, Jonas Mekas, Irving Blum, Henry Geldzahler, Susan Sontag, Timothy Baum.

Video Quartet (2002)
Crew: *Director-Editor* Christian Marclay. Originally commissioned by the San Francisco Museum of Art and the Musée d'Art Moderne Grand-Duc Jean, Luxembourg, with the support of the James Family Foundation. Edition of five, 4-channel video projection, four screens (approximately 8 feet by 10 feet), 14 minutes.

Bibliography

Books

— Anker, Steve (ed.): *Austrian Avant-Garde Cinema 1955–1999*. Sixpack Film, 1994.
— Arnheim, Rudolph: *Film as Art*. University of California Press, 1957.
— Arthur, Paul: *A Line of Sight: American Film Since 1945*. University of Minnesota Press, 2006.
— Bordwell, David: *Figures Traced in Light: On Cinematic Staging*. University of California Press, 2005.
— Brougher, Kerry and Olivia Mattis, Jeremy Strick, Ari Wiseman, Judith Zilczer: *Visual Music: Synaesthesia in Art and Music Since 1900*. Thames & Hudson/Hirshhorn Museum, 2005.
— Brougher, Kerry and Jonathan Crary, Bruce Jenkins, Kate Linker, Russell Ferguson (eds.): *Hall of Mirrors, Art and Film Since 1945*. MOCA/Monacelli Press, 1996.
— *Cinema Cinema: Contemporary Art and the Cinematic Experience*. Van Abbemuseum, Stedelijk, NAi Publishers, 1999.
— Danino, Nina and Michael Mazière: *The Undercut Reader: Critical Writing on Artist's Film and Video*. Wallflower Press, 2003.
— Dalle-Vacche, Angela: *Cinema and Painting: How Art Is Used in Film*. University of Texas Press, 1997.
— De Oliveira, Nicolas: *Installation Art in the New Millennium: Empire of the Senses*. Thames & Hudson, 2003.
— Dwoskin, Stephen: *Film Is: The International Free Cinema*. The Overlook Press, 1985.
— Foster, Stephen C.: *Hans Richter: Activism, Modernism, and the Avant-Garde*. MIT Press, 2003.
— Haller, Robert A. (ed.): *Galaxy: Avant-Garde Filmmakers Look Across Space and Time*. Anthology Film Archives, 2001.
— Haller, Robert A. (ed.): *First Light*. Anthology Film Archives, 1998.
— Hammond, Paul (ed.): *The Shadow and Its Shadow*. City Lights Books, 2000.
— Iles, Chrissie and Thomas Zummer: *Into the Light: The Projected Image in American Art 1964–1977*. Cantz Ostfildern/Harry Abrams, 2001.
— Jenkins, Janet: *In the Spirit of Fluxus*. Walker Art Center, 1993.
— Kearton, Nicola: *Art and Film*. Academy Group Ltd., 1996.
— Kilchesty, Albert (ed.): *Big as Life: An American History of 8mm Films*. Cinematograph, 1998.
— Michalka, Matthias (ed.): *X-Film Film Installation and Actions in the 1960s and 1970s*. Verlag der Buchhandlung, 2004. Raisonne/Abrams/Whitney Museum, 2006.
— Renan, Sheldon: *An Introduction to the American Underground Film*. E. P. Dutton, 1967.
— Rees, A. L.: *A History of Experimental Film and Video*. BFI Publishing, 1999.
— Rush, Michael: *New Media in Late 20th Century Art*. Thames & Hudson, 1998.
— Shaw, Jeffrey and Peter Weibel (eds.): *Future Cinema: The Cinematic Imaginary After Film*. ZKM/MIT Press, 2003.
— Sitney, P. Adams (ed.): *The Avant-Garde Film: A Reader of Theory and Criticism*. Anthology Film Archives, 1987.
— Sitney, P. Adams: *Modernist Montage: The Obscurity of Vision in Cinema and Literature*. Columbia University Press, 1990.
— Sitney, P. Adams: *Visionary Film: The American Avant-Garde 1943–2000*. Oxford University Press, 2002.
— Stauffacher, Frank: *Art in Cinema*. San Francisco Museum of Art, 1947.
— Vogel, Amos: *Film as a Subversive Art*. Weidenfeld & Nicholson/Random House, 1974.
— Wollen, Peter: *Making Time: Considering Time as a Material in Contemporary Video and Film*. Palm Beach Institute of Contemporary Art/DAP, 2000.
— Youngblood, Gene: *Expanded Cinema*. E. P. Dutton, 1970.

Additional Magazines and Periodicals Cited

Afterimage, Artforum, Art issues, ArtReview, BOMB, Canyon Cinema Catalog, CineAction, Cineaste, Cinema Journal, Film Criticism, Film Culture, Frieze, High Performance, Los Angeles Times, Millennium Film Journal, MoMA Circulating Film Catalog, New York Times, October, Parkett, Screen Notes, Spectator, Time Out (New York/London), *The Village Voice, Wide Angle*.

Program Notes

The American Cinematheque, Blum & Poe Gallery, Canyon Cinema, Center for Visual Music, Contemporary Projects at LACMA, Dia Center, Filmforum Los Angeles, The Film Society of Lincoln Center, The Goethe-Institut, UCLA's Hammer Museum, The Iota Center, Jack H. Skirball Film Series at REDCAT, LACE, MAK Center for Art and Architecture, Michael Kohn Gallery, MOCA, New York Film Festival, Other Cinema San Francisco, The San Francisco Cinematheque, Santa Monica Museum of Art, Shoshana Wayne Gallery, Tate Modern, UCLA Film and Television.

Websites

Artnet, Center for Visual Music, Chicago Reader, EAI, Fred Camper, Hi-beam, IMDB, Luxonline, Magill's Survey of Cinema, Masters of Cinema, Minorcinema, MIT, Revoir, Rhizome, Video Data Bank, Senses of Cinema, Variety.

Image Credits

Anthology = Anthology Film Archives, New York
BFI = British Film Institute Stills, Posters and Designs, London

Cover © Peter Mays, Courtesy the artist; 1 © The Estate of Bruce Conner, Courtesy the artist / Michael Kohn Gallery, Los Angeles; 2 © Paul and Damon McCarthy, Photo Ann-Marie Rounkle, Courtesy the artists / Hauser & Wirth, Zürich, London; 4/5 © Robert Nelson, Courtesy the artist / Mark Toscano; 6/7 © Bruce Elder, Courtesy Anthology; 8 © Embassy International Pictures, Courtesy BFI; 10top © Fernand Léger, Courtesy BFI; 10bottom © Le Film d'Art, Courtesy BFI; 11 © Fernand Léger, Courtesy BFI; 12t © Klein & Shamroy, Courtesy BFI; 12b © Pathé Frères, Courtesy BFI; 13t © Ivan Barnett, Courtesy BFI; 13b © Arturo González Producciones Cinematográficas, S.A, Constantin Film Produktion, Produzioni Europee Associati (PEA), Courtesy BFI; 14, 15 © Francis Brugière , Courtesy BFI; 16(2), 17(2) © Goskino., Courtesy BFI; 18 © Paul and Damon McCarthy, Photo Ann-Marie Rounkle, Courtesy the artists / Hauser & Wirth, Zürich, London; 20t © Roméo Bosetti, Courtesy BFI; 20b © Germaine Dulac, Courtesy BFI; 21t © 1926 Film Arts Guild, Courtesy BFI; 21b © Germaine Dulac, Courtesy BFI; 22 © Canyon Cinema, Film-Makers' Cooperative and Robert Nelson, Courtesy Anthology; 23t © Sidney Peterson, Courtesy BFI; 23bleft+bright © Sidney Peterson, Courtesy Anthology; 24 © Vicomte de Noailles, Photo Sacha Masour, Courtesy Anthology; 25(2) © Vicomte de Noailles, Photo Sacha Masour, Courtesy BFI; 26t © Hans Richter, Courtesy BFI; 26b © Walerian Borowczyk & Jan Lenica, Courtesy BFI; 27(2) © Athanor, Courtesy BFI; 28 © Isabelle Films, S.A.T.P.E.C., Courtesy BFI; 29t © Babylone Films, Courtesy BFI; 29b © Isabelle Films, S.A.T.P.E.C., Courtesy BFI; 30t © Paulette Phillips, Courtesy the artist / Diaz Contemporary, Toronto; 30bl+br © Roy Andersson Filmproduktion/Studio 24 Distribution, Courtesy Roy Andersson / Studio 24 Distribution; 31 © Nicolas Provost, Courtesy the artist; 32 © Marnie Weber, Courtesy the artist / Praz-Delavallade Gallery, Paris; 33t © Tracey Moffatt, Courtesy Victoria Miro Gallery, London; 33b © Hiraki Sawa, Courtesy James Cohan Gallery, New York; 34(4), 35 © Paul and Damon McCarthy, Photo Ann-Marie Rounkle, Courtesy the artists / Hauser & Wirth, Zürich, London; 36 © André Paulvé for DisCina, Courtesy BFI; 38t, 39 © The Estate of Gregory J. Markopoulos, Courtesy Anthology; 38b © The Estate of Gregory J. Markopoulos, Courtesy Anthology; 40t(2) © The Estate of Harry Smith and the Harry Smith Archives, Courtesy Harry Smith Archives and Rani Singh; 40b(2), 41 © Ed Emschwiller, Courtesy Anthology; 42(2), 43(2) © Kenneth Anger, Courtesy Walter Cassidy and Stuart Shave, Modern Art, London; 44(2) © Isaac Julien, Courtesy Victoria Miro Gallery, London; 45t © Willard Maas, Courtesy Anthology; 45b © Curtis Harrington, Courtesy BFI; 46, 47 © 2002 Matthew Barney, Photo Chris Winget, Courtesy Gladstone Gallery, New York; 48(3), 49(4) © and courtesy ABKCO Films; 50 © Peter Mays, Courtesy the artist; 51(2) © Len Lye Foundation, Courtesy Govett-Brewster Art Gallery and the New Zealand Film Archive; 52 © Oswell Blakeston, Francis Bruguière, Courtesy BFI; 53t+middle © The Elfriede Fischinger Trust, Courtesy Center for Visual Music, Los Angeles; 53b © Hans Richter, Courtesy BFI; 54(2), 55(2) © The Estate of John and James Whitney, Courtesy The Estate of John and James Whitney; 56t © James Davis, Courtesy Anthology; 56bl+br © Hy Hirsch, Courtesy BFI; 57t © Marie Menken, Courtesy Anthology; 57b © May Ellen Bute, Courtesy BFI; 58ml © Stephen Beck, Courtesy the artist; 58mr © Ian Helliwell, Courtesy the artist / LUX, London; 58bl+br © Woody Vasulka, Courtesy Woody and Steina Vasulka; 59(2) © Jeremy Blake Estate, Courtesy Feigen Contemporary Art, New York; 60(3), 61(3) © The Estate of Stan Brakhage, Courtesy the Estate of Stan Brakhage / Fred Camper; 62(3), 63 © Bruce Baillie, Courtesy the artist / Mark Toscano; 64(3) © Phil Solomon, Courtesy the artist; 65(2) © British Lion Film Corporation, Courtesy BFI; 66, 67 © Jordan Belson, Courtesy Center for Visual Music; 68 © Deutsche Vereinsfilm AG, FOX-Europa-Produktion, Courtesy BFI; 69 © Robert Florey, Courtesy BFI; 70(2) © Charles Sheeler, Courtesy BFI; 71, 72(2), 73 © VUFKU, Courtesy BFI; 74(2) © Erich Pommer for UFA, Courtesy BFI; 75(2) © Shirley Clarke, Courtesy BFI; 76(3), 77 © Ernie Gehr, Courtesy the artist; 78(2) © Robert Beavers, Courtesy the artist; 79t © Capi-Holland,

Still from 'The Holy Mountain' (1973)
The fool is about to meet the alchemist who will lead him on a journey of self-discovery.